Maryjeanne Vincent
775 Amador Ave
Seaside, CA 93955

THE STRANGE LIKENESS

Judy shivered as Peter fastened the chain around her neck.

A JUDY BOLTON Mystery

The Strange Likeness

BY

Kate Duvall and
Beverly Hatfield

Illustrated by
Marjorie Sutton Eckstein

Edited by
Lindsay Sutton Stroh

The title of this book, as well as
most of the characters and
settings, were created by

Margaret Sutton

APPLEWOOD BOOKS
Bedford, Massachusetts

Dedication

To the Phantom Friends
and Judy Bolton fans
all around the world

———————

For a complete list of titles in the Judy Bolton Mysteries,
please visit judybolton.awb.com

Thank you for purchasing an Applewood Book.
Applewood reprints America's lively classics—books
from the past that are still of interest to modern readers.

For a free copy of our current catalog, write to:

Applewood Books
P.O. Box 365
Bedford, MA 01730
www.awb.com

ISBN 978-1-4290-9321-7

PRINTED IN THE UNITED STATES OF AMERICA

Contents

CHAPTER I

Christmas Shopping

"CALL me Scrooge, but last-minute Christmas shopping is a hassle!" Honey, who held a bright red Brandt's Department Store bag in each hand, tossed her head in an unsuccessful attempt to flip a strand of dark blonde hair out of her eyes. "How do you manage to stay so cheerful, Judy?"

Judy took one of her sister-in-law's bags to carry. Her left hand free, Honey brushed the hair from her eyes, but she still looked a little grumpy.

"Shopping on Christmas Eve can be fun—I actually prefer it," Judy confessed. "It's exciting."

Honey sighed. "I'm not sure I have the holiday spirit this year. It's hard for me to find the right gift under pressure. I knew I should have bought Horace's gift sooner."

"Don't worry. I'm sure my brother will love whatever you give him," Judy reassured her. Horace Bolton loved everything about Grace Dobbs. Grace's nickname, "Honey," fit her perfectly, not just because of her honey-colored hair but also because of her sweet disposition.

"It's true," Judy said. "You could give him a lump of coal. If it came from you, it would be a diamond in his eyes."

And speaking of diamonds... But no, Judy's suspicions regarding Horace's Christmas gift to Honey were best left unspoken. The two girls had become best friends long before Judy Bolton had married Honey's brother, Peter Dobbs.

"Are you finished shopping?" Honey asked. "Wrapping gifts will probably take hours!"

Judy regarded her friend with concern. This frowning, unhappy girl was unlike the Honey she knew.

The sight of the escalator carrying an endless stream of children and parents to the upper floors gave Judy an idea. "Let's make one more stop," she told Honey and guided her through the crowd.

As soon as Honey realized where they were headed, she protested. "There's nothing interesting upstairs except the toy department. Peter hasn't started playing with model trains or teddy bears, has he?"

Despite her concern for Honey, Judy had to

smile. "Actually, I'd like to see Peter having fun with a train set. Lately he's been so serious."

The fact that Judy's husband had left his law practice and now worked for the FBI was a secret shared only with family and their closest friends. Peter's job made Judy proud, but she missed him when he went away on mysterious assignments that he was forbidden to discuss. Peter's boyish enthusiasm was one of the things that had first attracted Judy, and she wished he had more time to relax and have fun.

Today was a perfect example. It was Christmas Eve, and even Judy's father, Dr. Bolton, had closed his busy office to spend time with his family. Peter, however, had left on a last-minute assignment, and Judy knew better than to ask where he was going.

"Really, Judy, why are we going upstairs?" Honey persisted.

Judy was about to answer when she caught a glimpse of a male passenger on the adjoining escalator. He had a black scarf around his neck, completely covering his nose and mouth, but there was no mistaking the blue eyes that had gazed into hers a thousand times. Now, however, they looked right past her without recognition— or pretended to.

"Honey!" Judy grabbed her friend's arm as their escalator ascended and the other staircase went down. "Look! There's Peter!"

Honey turned to gape at the man's rapidly disappearing back. "Why didn't he say hello?"

Judy smiled at Honey's perplexed expression. "Can't you guess?"

"You're the detective," Honey replied. Ever since Judy's high school days she had demonstrated a natural flair for solving mysteries. Today she still looked like a teenager, her auburn curls held back with a festive green ribbon.

"It's simple," Judy said as she stepped off the escalator. "Peter wanted to do some last-minute shopping. We didn't tell him we were going to Brandt's, so he didn't expect to run into us. When he saw us on the escalator, he pulled up his scarf and kept quiet," Judy laughed happily. "As if I wouldn't recognize my own husband!"

"And my own brother," Honey added and smiled for the first time that afternoon.

Both girls were in considerably brighter moods as they entered the toy department on the second floor. Santa, seated on his red plush throne, listened as a toddler whispered in his ear.

"I wonder what she's wishing for," said Judy. "Perhaps a doll like this one." She reached up to touch the delicate lace on its bonnet. The baby doll had soft blonde curls, blue eyes, and a pug nose just like Peter's.

"Go ahead, buy her," urged Honey. "You can save her for your daughter someday."

"No, I'd better not. I may wind up with a bunch of boys!"

"Boys are nice, too," Honey sighed wistfully. "My brother Mike was an adorable baby." Honey rarely talked about her childhood. When Peter and Honey's mother died, Marie Vincenzo, the landlady, had placed Peter in an orphanage and sent a telegram to the family. When Peter's grandmother went to New York to get her grandchildren, she was told that the baby girl, named Grace after her mother, had died. This was not true. Mrs. Vincenzo had kept the baby girl, renamed her Rose, and raised her with her own sons. Mr. and Mrs. Dobbs adopted their grandson, changing his name to Peter Dobbs. It wasn't until sixteen years later that Mr. and Mrs. Dobbs learned that their granddaughter was alive. Only then did the young girl learn that Marie Vincenzo was not her real mother.

"I never had a real doll. Once I drew some paper dolls, and Mike and I cut them out and played with them," Honey recalled, her eyes clouding with sad memories. "Mike's brothers teased us and tore the paper dolls into pieces. I was afraid of the older Vincenzo boys, but I loved little Mike."

Judy put her arm around Honey and steered her away from the doll shelf. "Try to forget about the Vincenzos. I have an idea. Let's stop and eat something. Brandt's tearoom is sure to cheer you up."

"Last week I dined here with Lois," Judy said after the girls were seated. "She treated me to cinnamon rolls and spiced tea."

"That sounds good," Honey replied as a waitress approached their table. Judy's thoughts drifted to their friends, Lois Farringdon-Pett and her brother, Arthur, who was now married to Lorraine Lee. Although the Farringdon-Petts were descendants of the founder of the city and lived in a mansion, Judy was no longer in awe of them or their wealth.

"Lois called me as soon as she came home for her college break," said Honey. "I think she is lonely with Arthur and Lorraine in Europe for a year. Mr. and Mrs. Lee will be feeling lonesome too with their only child so far away at Christmas. No matter how much family you have, when someone is missing, the holidays are not the same."

A familiar voice interrupted their conversation. Judy turned around to see Lois carrying a gaily decorated tin box.

"Merry Christmas!" Lois greeted them cheerfully.

"Please join us," Honey invited.

"I would love to, but I have to pack. This morning Mother and Father surprised me with an early Christmas present—tickets to London! We're going with the Lees to see Lorraine and Arthur. I came to pick up our favorite cinnamon rolls to take along."

"What fun!" Judy enthused. "London sounds so Christmassy to me—like stepping into the pages of *A Christmas Carol*."

"Maybe I should reread it on the flight over. I wish I could join you, but I have one more errand before I return to packing."

"Tell Arthur and Lorraine hello for us, and Merry Christmas!" said Judy.

Judy turned to comment on the Farringdon-Petts' plans but stopped when she saw the expression on Honey's face. The encounter had obviously upset her best friend.

"Tell me what's wrong, Honey," Judy said gently. "I may not be able to solve your problems, but at least I can sympathize."

"Talking about people not being together for Christmas reminded me again of a letter I received yesterday." Honey paused, her eyes filling with tears. "I'm afraid I've lost my brother!"

CHAPTER II

The Shoplifter

HONEY brought out a pale blue envelope from her purse and handed it facedown to Judy. To Judy's surprise, the seal was unbroken. How could an unopened letter upset Honey? Turning it over, Judy checked the return address. It was from Honey but addressed to Mike Vincenzo and had been stamped "Address Unknown."

At the same time Honey was restored to the Dobbs family seven years ago, Mike Vincenzo broke away from his family and went to live on a nearby farm. He was given room and board in exchange for his chores. After high school, he found a paying job on a farm in Bradford, an hour from Farringdon. At first Peter drove Honey to visit Mike, but when Peter's work kept him too busy,

Horace had taken over. Since Honey had received her driver's license, she had gone on her own to visit the young man who still seemed like her real brother. Honey didn't consider Mrs. Vincenzo's other sons as her brothers, but she was close to the boy she had practically raised.

"My work at Dean Studios has kept me busy, so I haven't gone to see Mike recently," Honey admitted. "I wanted to tell him things that were too private to be shared in a phone call, so I wrote him a long letter." Honey fought back tears as she struggled to continue. "Now my Christmas card with the letter has been returned, and I don't know how to find him." As Honey spoke, a dim picture formed in Judy's mind of a skinny, dark-haired boy who called Honey "Sis" although she wasn't really his sister.

Judy looked closer at the blue envelope that had been sent in care of Sam Smollett, Bradford, Pennsylvania.

"This doesn't mean something bad has happened," Judy pointed out. "Mike could be away at college, or living on his own, or even in the army."

Honey shook her head. "He wouldn't. Not without telling me."

"You're right," Judy sympathized. "You must be worried sick about him."

"He probably thinks I've forgotten him or don't care anymore. Once he wondered if my new family would take me away from him." Honey's voice trembled. "I haven't phoned him for a couple of months."

"Do you want me to help you find Mike?" Judy offered. "You have his last known address, and that's a pretty big clue."

"You're right, Judy. Even if Mike has moved away, the Smolletts should know how to reach him. Will you go with me to Bradford so I can talk to them in person? I don't have to work next week because Mr. Dean is closing the studio through New Year's Day."

"Sure," Judy agreed. "After Christmas, we can make the trip whenever you want."

Judy's promise did not relieve Honey's worried expression or her fidgeting with her teacup and plate. Her friend's pinched, pale face had the look of a rabbit in a trap. When Honey didn't volunteer more information, Judy decided to be blunt. "What else is bothering you?"

"Worrying about Mike has made me think about growing up with the Vincenzo family. Maybe Horace doesn't know the real me and how the Vincenzos influenced me," said Honey.

"Horace knows you and loves you just the way you are," Judy assured her.

"I want to believe that."

"Then do," said Judy. "If something unknown happens in the future, your love and faith in each other will see you through. That's how I feel about Peter."

"You're right. I should have known that talking with you would help," said Honey. "Now that we have a plan for finding Mike, I feel a little better. I'm ready to tackle the rest of my list."

The girls settled their check and headed back to the toy department.

"You've given me an idea. I'm going to buy a toy train engine for Peter," said Judy. "Perhaps buying part of a train set will become a new Christmas tradition for us."

"Oh, I like that...and I see something that Horace is sure to like. I'll meet you beside the train display in fifteen minutes."

Honey rushed off, and Judy spent the time selecting an old-fashioned train engine. At the appointed time, Honey returned carrying yet another Brandt's shopping bag, and the two friends stepped onto the descending escalator.

As the stairs carried them down, the girls had a magnificent view of the ground floor of Brandt's. Enormous green tinsel wreaths hung from the ceiling, and the counters were draped in garlands of red and gold. A group of carolers was gathered around a lamppost on a platform decorated to look like a snowy street scene. They looked as though they were part of a Christmas card, and their voices floated throughout the store.

"Look, there's Peter again," Honey said.

Sure enough, Peter was by the jewelry counter. Judy saw a young salesclerk unlock the case and hand him a necklace set with shimmering blue stones. The escalator dipped lower, hiding their view of the jewelry department.

"Let's circle around and see what Peter's up to," Honey proposed when they reached the first floor. She pointed to one of the golden Christmas trees situated at intervals on the sales floor. "We can hide behind that tree near the jewelry counter and peek through the branches."

Judy knew she should leave and wait for Peter to surprise her at home, but curiosity got the better of her. Besides, she didn't want to spoil Honey's cheerful mood. Peter didn't turn around as they tiptoed past and ducked behind the shiny gold tree with green ornaments.

"He's looking at a diamond pendant," whispered Honey. "Do you think it's your present, Judy?"

"I don't know. It is gorgeous," Judy whispered back. They watched as the salesclerk brought other items out of the glass case, including a set of ruby earrings.

"Why is Peter looking at rubies? Oh, we really need to leave now, Honey. I feel guilty spying on him. Whatever he buys, I don't want to spoil his Christmas surprise."

The girls were leaving their hiding place when

a commotion caused them to look back.

"Miss! Over here!" An attractive woman with long black hair and wearing a bright pink coat waved to the jewelry clerk. "I want this bracelet, and I'm in a hurry!" Tottering on impossibly high heels, the woman reached into a beaded purse and pulled out a handful of bills.

As the woman approached the counter, she suddenly slipped and sprawled in the aisle with a loud shriek. The money flew from her hands and rained down around her. The jewelry clerk and several shoppers rushed to assist her as she shouted threats about suing Brandt's. Her loud voice and striking appearance commanded attention.

"That woman is causing a distraction so her partner can shoplift," said Honey. "I'm sure those bills are all ones." The young woman in pink was creating quite a commotion. From a distance it was impossible to tell the bills' denominations.

"I know this con," Honey continued.

"Are you saying that woman is a criminal, and you know her?" asked Judy in astonishment.

"Not her. It. The con game," Honey said. "Trust me, the woman is an amateur. I could do a better job myself—did you forget that I'm a well-trained thief?"

Judy knew Mrs. Vincenzo was an expert shoplifter who had taught her children to steal. Judy was again reminded that Honey must carry a heavy burden of troubling memories.

"Ma called it 'shopping.' Sometimes the boys stole for themselves. One of the boys bragged about sneaking a coloring book out of a drugstore under his shirt until Tony pointed out that he'd forgotten to steal the crayons." Tony was the oldest Vincenzo son. Honey shook her head as if she were shaking away the memory.

"Can you imagine how the people standing here would react if they knew I was shoplifting before I knew how to read?" asked Honey. "It would be even worse if our friends knew. The only ones I ever told were Peter and your family."

Judy's eyes returned to the crowd surrounding the woman in pink, expecting to see Peter among the people who were helping the woman to her feet. Where was he? Judy looked all around and caught a faraway glimpse of Peter headed out the door, his stride easy and confident. She turned back to the jewelry counter and saw the salesclerk frantically looking through the glass cases. The necklaces Peter had been holding in his hands were both gone!

CHAPTER III

Christmas Eve

HONEY, obviously unaware of the missing jewelry, began perusing a shelf of scarves, but Judy was too troubled to think about shopping. It didn't make sense! Peter wouldn't walk away from someone in trouble, and in her heart, Judy knew he would never, ever steal anything, but he had been holding both necklaces in his hands just moments ago. There had to be an explanation!

Determined to put her emotions aside and think things through, Judy reviewed recent events and conversations until she remembered something that had happened a month ago. A man who was driving too fast for the Dry Brook Hollow roads had almost hit Judy's cat, Blackberry. Judy had caught a fleeting glance of the driver as he sped away, and he looked just like Peter. Later Peter confided that he had a slight resemblance to a man under investigation by the FBI, and he might be asked to take his place. Was this shop-lifter the other man, or was Peter playing along with a group of con artists in order to trap them? Was that why he had to report to work on Christ-mas Eve?

Witnessing a theft and not being able to report it, or even tell her best friend, frustrated Judy. She was anxious to talk with Peter. At least she hoped they could talk about what she had seen. If Peter had stolen the necklaces as part of his current as-signment, everything would be confidential. If the thief had not been Peter, at least she would be able to tell him about what she suspected. Now Judy was as eager to leave the store as Honey had been earlier. Unfortunately, Honey had other plans.

"Do you mind if we go back upstairs?" asked Honey.

Judy could not imagine why. They had al-ready been in the toy department and surely Hon-ey hadn't decided to buy linens or furniture on Christmas Eve.

Honey must have sensed Judy's reticence be-cause she explained, "I want to buy some pastries for tomorrow morning. It will save me from bak-ing tonight. Grandma and Grandpa always ap-preciate a special Christmas breakfast."

Judy complied. She had no choice because

she couldn't tell Honey what she suspected. A few more minutes shouldn't matter, but it turned out to be a much longer wait. The line of customers stretched the entire length of Brandt's bakery counter. Thankfully, they were in a jolly mood and exchanged gift ideas while they waited. Two saleswomen, wearing velvet Santa hats trimmed with fur, kept the line moving or the wait would have been much longer. After buying half a dozen pastries, Honey stopped at the candy counter.

Judy was determined not to let Honey know her concerns. "Two boxes of chocolates? You must think my brother is awfully sweet," she teased after Honey had made her purchase.

Honey laughed. "Horace keeps chocolate in his desk drawer at work, but don't let him know I told you. He would never buy such exquisite chocolates for himself. The second box will make a good gift for Mike when we find him."

Judy felt like she and Honey had changed places. Honey's grouchy mood had dissipated, and now she was infused with the holiday spirit. Judy, on the other hand, struggled to appear in good spirits and hide her worry and impatience. That task became even harder as the escalator brought the girls to the first floor. One Farringdon police officer was questioning the clerk at the jewelry counter while another was examining the glass case. Mr. Brandt, rarely seen outside his office, was standing with the group.

"I was right," said Honey. "I knew that woman was helping a shoplifter. I wonder what was stolen and who her partner was."

Judy was afraid she knew who the partner was, but she certainly wasn't going to tell Honey or the police officers. Peter was the only one she wanted to talk with, and she wanted to talk with him now!

It seemed like hours before Judy was back on Grove Street. Her mother opened the front door and enveloped her daughter in a hug.

"Merry Christmas, Mom. Is Peter here yet?" Judy asked anxiously as she set down her shopping bags and slipped out of her coat.

She hoped Peter would arrive in time for them to talk before the Christmas Eve dinner with their families. When Peter had dropped her at the Dobbs apartment that morning, he hadn't said when he would return.

"I have some disappointing news, dear," Mrs. Bolton said. "Peter called, and he won't be here until sometime Christmas Day. So I've called his grandparents, and we agreed that we'll be together tomorrow afternoon."

Judy sighed with frustration. Peter needed to know about what she had seen.

"Mom, I need to call the Field Office and leave him a message."

Judy made a beeline for the upstairs phone and dialed the familiar number. She asked the woman who answered to have Peter return her call as soon as possible.

"Is Horace home?" Judy asked her mother as she came downstairs.

"I don't expect him for another hour. He and your father went out to select the perfect Christmas tree," Mrs. Bolton replied. "I have some wrapping paper and ribbon set out on the table so you can wrap your purchases while we wait for them."

Thankfully Judy didn't have much to wrap, because she spent more time thinking than wrapping. The morning's events continued to plague her.

Judy had to admit she had not seen much of the man's face or his hair. Many men wore gray trench coats identical to Peter's. Those intense blue eyes and the way he walked had made her sure he was Peter, but now she wasn't certain. The man she loved and had married would never abandon someone who might be hurt or leave the scene of a crime. That is unless he was working undercover, and if he was, she knew she should not get involved or discuss it with anyone else.

What should she do? "Use your head, Judy girl." Her father's often-repeated advice echoed in her mind.

If the thief wasn't Peter, then it was someone who looked like him, so the first question was "Who would look like Peter?" A family member seemed likely. Judy had met several of Peter's aunts and uncles as well as cousins on the Dobbs side of the family, but she had never met any of Peter's paternal relatives. She reviewed what little she knew.

Peter's father, James Thompson, had a stepmother named Vine and two younger half-brothers by Vine. At age eighteen, James Thompson eloped with Grace Dobbs, and the couple moved to Brooklyn, a borough of New York City. Peter had been born a year later. All that was known about the couple's life was contained in some old letters Judy discovered in the attic when her family moved into the house where Vine Thompson had lived, and where she had been murdered. Apparently James had left Brooklyn seeking work, and Grace sent him letters in care of his stepmother. James never saw the letters his wife sent him because he died in a car accident. Since Vine didn't bother to contact her stepson's wife, Grace never knew the sad fate of her husband, and she died impoverished, thinking James had abandoned her.

Chief Kelly of the Farringdon Police Department had told Judy that Vine Thompson's older son was a criminal who was sentenced to life in the state penitentiary. Judy had caught a glimpse of the younger son when he was caught stealing a trunk from the Bolton attic during a Halloween party. This second son had been found guilty of several robberies and sent to prison. Had some other branch of the Thompson family produced a criminal who resembled Peter?

Judy's thoughts were interrupted by Mrs. Bolton entering the room with a battered cardboard box. "I had Horace bring these down from the attic this morning."

Judy raised the lid and looked down on a large collection of homemade ornaments crafted by Judy and Horace when they were in elementary school.

"I am so glad I found these in Mother's attic," said Mrs. Bolton. She pulled out a crocheted snowflake and a knitted wreath. "I remember your grandma making these while she waited for her pies to bake. You know her hands were never idle."

Judy smiled at the memory of her grandmother sitting by the fireplace doing her handwork. A sturdier box had been placed on the coffee table, and Judy reached into it and retrieved a hand-blown glass tree. The tiny ornament had bits of red and green at the tips of its glass branches. "I remember purchasing this at Brandt's our first Christmas in Farringdon. Honey and I had such a good time that day," Judy recalled fondly.

"And here is the glass reindeer Horace chose," Mrs. Bolton reminisced, holding up the little ornament.

Just then Judy's father and brother arrived with a freshly cut evergreen tied to the roof of Dr. Bolton's sedan.

"Hand me the first string of lights," Horace called from the top step of the ladder after the tree was in place. After the lights, each ornament was carefully placed on the evergreen's branches. When Horace plugged in the colored lights, the family stood back to admire the transformation.

Mrs. Bolton breathed a contented sigh. "A real old-fashioned Christmas tree!"

"How about some old-fashioned cookies? Don't I smell gingerbread?" asked Horace.

"There's a plateful in the kitchen," answered Mrs. Bolton.

Horace took Judy's arm and led her into the privacy of the kitchen with him. "What's bothering you, Sis? I can tell you aren't in the Christmas mood."

"I'm just anxious to talk to Peter. It's going to be so hard to wait until tomorrow to see him."

"If after two years, you still can't bear to be parted from Peter, then that's a good advertisement for marriage."

"It's not that," said Judy. "I need to talk with him."

"That is still a good advertisement for marriage. You haven't run out of things to discuss."

"We certainly have a lot to discuss today. I wish Peter would hurry back."

Horace patted Judy's shoulder before bounding up the stairs. In a moment, he returned wearing fresh clothes and left the house. He didn't say anything, but Judy suspected where he was going and what would take place. Tomorrow might be more than a Christmas celebration between the Dobbses and the Boltons.

CHAPTER IV

Unexpected Presents

THE eight-foot evergreen dominated the Boltons' living room and filled the room with a spicy fragrance as the Bolton and the Dobbs families gathered on Christmas afternoon. Gaily wrapped gifts peeked out from under the lowest boughs. Horace slipped his arm around Honey. "That's the kind of tree I want in our living room someday." Honey smiled back, and a sweet understanding seemed to pass between them.

Judy was pleased to see the exchange. Contrary to what she had expected, Honey had not been wearing an engagement ring when she and her grandparents had arrived. Both Honey and Horace had been unusually quiet while they sipped eggnog and everyone waited for Peter.

Judy noticed that there didn't seem to be any tension between the two. Maybe Horace had only asked Mr. Dobbs for Honey's hand in marriage, and Honey would receive her ring today. Judy had spotted a small box under the fresh-cut evergreen. The size and shape indicated jewelry, and Judy recognized Brandt's distinctive gold-foil gift-wrap.

Her thoughts were interrupted by a cold blast of air as Peter came in with Blackberry in one arm and presents in the other.

"Brrr! It feels like the North Pole out there," Peter shivered. "Merry Christmas, everyone! I'm sorry I delayed our celebration."

"We're glad to see you, son," Dr. Bolton greeted him.

"I'm just thankful that you got away from work," Mrs. Bolton added. "I'll put those gifts under the tree for you."

"It was pretty overcast earlier. Any sign of snow?" asked Grandpa Dobbs.

"I thought I felt a flake or two, but it was wishful thinking," Peter answered.

"Judy, why don't you take Peter to the kitchen and pour him some eggnog," Honey suggested. Judy suspected that Honey knew she wanted to be alone with Peter.

As soon as she closed the kitchen door, Judy asked, "Were you at Brandt's yesterday? Honey and I thought we saw you."

"No, but why would that worry you?"

"You can always tell when something is bothering me," said Judy. She didn't mind Peter being able to read her so easily, as she never intended to hide anything from him. Before she could explain, her mother appeared in the doorway and announced, "Time for presents!"

Peter squeezed Judy's hand and whispered, "We'll discuss this later," and followed his mother-in-law back to living room.

Judy wished she could change course as easily. Now that Peter was back, she couldn't stop thinking about the shoplifter and replaying the scene at Brandt's over and over in her mind. And yet, seeing Peter erased any doubts, no matter how slight, that he would be involved in anything dishonest. If the shoplifter wasn't Peter, who was he? Judy thought of all the possibilities she had pondered Christmas Eve until she realized she had missed a question that Grandma Dobbs had asked. She must turn her thoughts back to Christmas.

When would Horace give Honey her ring? Judy wondered. Her brother was a private person and nervous about public displays of feelings. Horace knew Honey wouldn't want a lot of fuss either. Would he give the ring to Honey first to get it over with or would he put it off until the end of the evening? Judy glanced at her brother to see if she could decide his strategy. He didn't look nervous, and Honey didn't look as if she were expecting something to happen. Had Judy misread the situation? She looked under the tree again. Yes, the gold-wrapped box must be jewelry.

"It's the men's turn to start this year, youngest to oldest," said Mrs. Bolton. So each gift could be admired by the group, they always took turns opening presents.

"That means Horace is first," said Honey, who was pleased with the arrangement. "Start with my present."

Horace quickly unwrapped a Scrabble game.

"So that's what Honey bought in the toy department," Judy said. "Let's all play tonight."

"Watch out," chuckled Mr. Dobbs. "Any girl who can win a community spelling bee at age fifteen should be a whiz at Scrabble." Judy would always remember the event Peter's grandfather mentioned, and it wasn't because she had won a spelling bee. It was the last party held in Roulsville before the flood. The next day the dam had broken, and the majority of the townspeople had lost their homes. They would have lost their lives if it hadn't been for Horace's bravery. Moments before the dam broke, Horace had risked his life to ride a frisky colt through the town and warn the people to move to higher ground.

"Don't sell an author short," said Dr. Bolton. "As much time as Horace has spent writing for the the *Daily Herald* and working on his novel at night, he should give Judy some good competition."

"What's this about a novel?" asked Grandma Dobbs.

"I don't like to count my chickens before they're hatched," Horace responded. "I've been playing around with some of Judy's adventures in order to make them into detective stories."

"Here's part two of your gift," said Honey, handing Horace a small package. Horace unwrapped a small book and held it up for everyone to see. "Don't worry, Honey made sure that I would have an advantage at Scrabble. She included a book of game strategy."

The next gift to be unwrapped, the toy train engine, pleased Peter, and even before Judy could mention it, he suggested adding to the set every Christmas.

"Setting up a train village underneath the Christmas tree is such a nice tradition for parents and children to share," added Mrs. Bolton with a twinkle in her eye, and Judy had to smile at her mother's obvious hint. When the time came, Judy knew her folks would be loving grandparents.

The next package was for Dr. Bolton. It was a pair of plush slippers, and he immediately kicked off his loafers and snuggled his feet into them. An ornate bow with a sprig of holly decorated a square package, and the tag read, "To Grandma and Grandpa, with love from Honey." When the wrapping was removed, a lovely framed watercolor was revealed.

"Oh, Honey, you've painted my favorite chair! And it shows that lovely vase you gave us too. I'll treasure this!" Mrs. Dobbs exclaimed. Clearly pleased with Honey's original painting, the Dobbses passed their gift around for everyone to admire.

"I told Honey that if she painted another picture like she has in previous years, I wanted to open it here for everyone to see," said Mr. Dobbs.

"Here's a present with Honey's name," said Mrs. Bolton as she reached for a rectangular box not quite covered with wrapping paper. Judy smiled to herself—it didn't take a detective to recognize her brother's gift-wrapping skills.

"Great minds think alike," announced Mr. Dobbs when Honey opened a game with a painting on the cover.

"You buy and sell works of art," Horace explained as Honey opened the box and pulled out the playing pieces. "The person with the greatest fortune in cash and valuable art wins."

"What a lovely idea," said Mrs. Dobbs, who was sitting beside her granddaughter. She reached over and picked out a card. "I love this picture of a mother bathing her child's feet."

"That's by Mary Cassatt," said Honey. "She painted many pictures of mothers and children although she never had children of her own."

Honey's grandmother flipped the card over and read the back. "You're right, Honey. It is by

Mary Cassatt. When we play this game, you can teach us about art."

"We'll have our own private art teacher," Mr. Dobbs said with obvious pride.

"This card shows a painting of some customers in a diner late at night—it looks so barren and lonely," Judy observed.

"That's one of Edward Hopper's most famous works," Honey told them. "Look how he created an ominous mood, contrasting the harsh electric light with the darkness of the city street."

"I'd rather have a painting of Joe's Diner in Roulsville—the mood is much friendlier," laughed Peter.

Judy gave her husband's hand an affectionate squeeze, remembering Peter's fumbling but sweet marriage proposal over a lunch of hamburgers at a picnic table at Joe's place. It reminded her again of her hopes for Horace and Honey, and Judy looked forward to the moment the gold-wrapped box from Brandt's would be retrieved from under the Christmas tree.

To Judy's surprise, Peter picked up the tiny package instead of Horace. As he handed it to her, Judy realized that she had not opened anything yet. She had been so caught up in the presents others were giving and receiving that she had not thought about herself. Even now, instead of wondering what the package contained, she wondered why Horace wasn't giving Honey a similar box.

Judy glanced under the tree to make sure. Yes, this was the only small package.

Still confused, Judy unwrapped the box, lifted the lid and gasped in astonishment. Resting on a bed of blue velvet, a diamond pendant glittered. Judy stared, speechless, as frozen as the icy blue-white stone.

"Kind of takes your breath away, doesn't it?" Peter's voice was gentle as he lifted the silver chain. It looked like an icicle, reflecting the light from the Christmas tree. Judy shivered as Peter fastened the chain around her neck. She could only think of the shoplifting scene at Brandt's. Her present was identical to one of the stolen necklaces!

CHAPTER V

Frozen Tears

JUDY didn't know what to say about this unexpected present. Her face must have reflected her
confusion, because Peter hurried to explain.

"I know it's an unusual necklace, Angel, but
you are the one who inspired it."

"Me?" Judy was baffled. "How could I in-
spire a necklace?"

"I was afraid I would forget the details, so I
asked Helen Brandt to write them down," said
Peter and handed Judy a note. Judy shook her
head numbly. Helen was the heir to the Brandt
family fortune, and a good friend as well, but
why would Peter discuss the necklace with her?
Judy unfolded the monogrammed stationery and
silently read the note.

December 20th

Dear Judy,

If you are reading this then you must already have the Frozen Tears Pendant. Remember when you solved the mystery of the haunted fountain on my family's estate? Afterwards, I remembered how you compared diamonds to frozen tears. The phrase stuck in my mind. I began dreaming of a line of romantic diamond jewelry. It seemed like a winning concept—Frozen Tears, exclusively at Brandt's Department Store. We started with a few pieces, and they were more successful than I ever imagined. I saw Peter the afternoon he was Christmas shopping and suggested a Frozen Tears necklace. I could tell he was hesitant, but the next day he came back and picked out a pendant. I may have made the suggestion, but Peter looked at all the jewelry and chose this necklace himself.

Since the original idea was yours, I want to thank you in person. Let's have lunch together once the holidays are over.

Fondly,
Helen

Judy was relieved. This was not the same necklace she had seen yesterday at the jewelry counter. She looked up and saw her family's expectant faces, so Judy read the note aloud.

"Oh, Judy, that's a real treasure," Grandma Dobbs remarked when Judy finished reading the letter.

More gifts were exchanged, and after the last present was opened, Honey went to help Mrs. Bolton in the kitchen. Blackberry was playing with the discarded wrapping paper and chasing strands of ribbon, much to the delight of Peter's grandparents. Horace and Dr. Bolton were examining the toy train engine. With everyone busy, Judy had a chance to be alone with her husband.

Peter could always read Judy's face and must have sensed her unease when she opened the box. However, his next words showed he misunderstood and thought she didn't like the design.

"If you decide you want a different necklace, exchange it. My feelings won't be hurt. Any Frozen Tears jewelry will remind me of your bravery in swimming through the Brandt's fountain and how thankful I was when you recovered from pneumonia."

"It isn't that I don't like the gift, Peter, it's just . . ." Judy didn't know where to begin. Again, Peter misunderstood her hesitancy in accepting the gift.

"It may seem like an extravagant gift, but your engagement ring is an heirloom from Grandma, so I never had a chance to buy you a diamond,"

Peter explained. "This diamond is just from me, a way to express how much I love you. And it's extra special because you inspired it."

Judy smiled up into Peter's dear face, but he saw that her gray eyes were still troubled. "What is really bothering you?" he asked.

That was all it took for the whole story to tumble out.

Peter listened patiently and then said, "This is very helpful, but there's not much I can share with you until I get permission. I'll be right back." Peter phoned from Dr. Bolton's office before he rejoined Judy in the kitchen.

"Let's take a drive," Peter suggested.

Judy grabbed her coat from the closet while Peter told Mrs. Bolton that they were going for a drive.

"We won't be long. I just want some time alone with Peter," Judy explained before following Peter to their black car, nicknamed the Beetle. If Peter wanted a private place to talk, that meant he might be allowed to share confidential information.

Peter drove down Grove Street without speaking. Maybe driving helped him think about what he wanted to say.

Judy tried to push her concerns away and let the sights and sounds of Christmas soothe her. As the sun set, outside lights came on at various houses. The sight of gaily decorated Christmas trees twinkling in people's windows reminded Judy of childhood Christmases at Grandma and Grandpa Smeed's farmhouse. She had always looked forward to seeing their tree with its old-fashioned decorations glowing a welcome from its place in the bay window on Christmas Day.

"Taking a drive helped, Peter," Judy said. "Looking at the streets all dressed up for Christmas makes me think everything in the world will turn out the way it should."

Peter waited until he had driven another block before he spoke. "The man you saw yesterday was most likely the man we suspect of investment fraud. We didn't know that he was also stealing jewelry, but it certainly makes sense. Following this angle may be the key to arresting him, since gathering evidence for a charge of defrauding investors can take a long time. Because of your report, I'm allowed to share some information."

"Does he look just like you, Peter?"

"You thought so, didn't you?"

"Yes, especially because of his blue eyes," said Judy. "Most of his face was covered by a scarf, and his back was towards me during the robbery."

"It's really only a slight resemblance, but people who don't know us well could be fooled." said Peter.

"Cousin Roxy and I look and even sound alike," Judy observed, remembering the time she and her look-alike cousin had changed places. "Is his voice like yours?" she asked.

"We haven't heard his voice. Two reports made to the FBI described a person who looked similar to me. I might have been a suspect if I hadn't been on an assignment with other agents on those days. As you know, the agency has to be especially careful and hold its agents to the highest standards."

"Honey saw him at the jewelry counter, but she didn't see him take the necklace," said Judy. "She thinks you hid your face so we wouldn't know you were Christmas shopping."

"I'll need to tell her and your family about the situation because I don't want this man to discover his resemblance to me and use it to deceive people. I have permission to do so. However, I don't want to alarm anyone, because this man doesn't have any history of violence. In fact, he's reported to be very charming, which helps him convince people to entrust him with their savings. I can't tell you the details. You just need to know enough to be alert."

"Will you be taking his place?" asked Judy.

"That's unlikely. We're revising our strategy now that we know about the shoplifting aspect. We didn't know the man was back in this area, so that news is important. He's given us the slip several times."

A comfortable silence rested between them as Peter continued to drive. They took turns pointing out light displays to each other. The pine trees and the tall barberry hedge in front of the elegant Farringdon-Pett mansion were decorated with sparkling white lights, and a huge green wreath festooned with red ribbon hung on the stone entrance gate. From the street, the only part of the mansion Judy could see were the tops of its palatial towers.

Judy momentarily put the disturbing events behind her until she remembered the possible family connections she had thought about while unpacking ornaments on Christmas Eve.

"Something else has been bothering me, Peter. The man acted like you. I don't mean stealing the necklace, but the way he carried his shoulders and stepped off the escalator. He had your stride."

"That bothers us, too. It is almost as if he has studied me. People don't notice those things about themselves, but another agent pointed it out. I can see siblings having the same mannerisms or a parent and child, but not strangers."

"Do you remember how it felt to learn you have similar mannerisms and the same stride as this suspect?" asked Judy. "I just received an eerie reminder of the strange likeness between the two of you," said Judy.

"What do you mean?" asked Peter.

"You both chose the same necklace. The one you gave me looks identical to the one that was stolen."

"Helen doesn't have that many designs, so it's not improbable for us to pick the same one," said Peter. "Does it bother you that the style is the same?"

"It did when I opened the box," admitted Judy, "but I love the fact that you chose it for me and the story of the Frozen Tears. The point I am trying to make is that the thief could be related to you. We know very little about your father's living relatives, only that his half-brothers are in prison. Before we knew Honey was your sister, she reminded me of you. Do you remember the day you brought over your parents' love letters for us to read? You and Honey were standing together, and I noticed how her eyes and yours are the same. Both of you have eyes that dance when you laugh. I thought about that moment after we learned Honey was your sister."

Peter was silent for a few moments, his brow wrinkled in concentration. "When I first joined the FBI, the agency did a confidential background check that included my family history. My superiors have access to that report, but I've never seen it. For all I know, they are already checking to see if our man might be a relative. I have to admit that I thought about it myself in the very beginning."

"I don't know of any young men who look like you on the Dobbs side of the family," Judy mused. "The Thompson side is a mystery."

"I'll ask Mr. Trent if the FBI is investigating that possibility," Peter said. "Now let's get back to our family Christmas."

When they returned from the drive, they found Honey, Mrs. Bolton, and Mrs. Dobbs playing the game Horace had given Honey. The older women were more interested in hearing Honey's comments about the art cards than in taking their turns. Honey was clearly enjoying herself. Horace came to stand next to Judy and looked thoughtful as he watched the players.

"Your present was certainly a hit," said Judy. "You understand Honey better than I do."

"Maybe, but not as well as I want to," Horace responded.

"Is that why you didn't give her an engagement ring for Christmas?" Judy blurted out.

"No. I love her and want to marry her," Horace responded. Judy was glad he didn't chide her for being nosy.

"I didn't mean to pry. I just expected you to give Honey a ring and said what I was thinking," explained Judy.

"I don't mind you asking. Honey can confide in you if she wants."

Judy nodded and decided not to say anything else. Horace looked over to where the other men had gathered. Grandpa Dobbs was reminiscing about a toy store from his childhood.

"I think your present was a hit, too," said

Horace with a grin.

"Do you think Peter really liked it?" asked Judy.

Before Horace could respond the phone rang, and Judy went to answer it.

"Peter, it's for you," Judy called.

Peter hurried into the kitchen. Judy handed him the receiver but couldn't resist lingering. His face betrayed no emotion as he listened and said "yes" or "no" at intervals, but when he replaced the phone and turned to her, his expression spoke volumes. Judy didn't have to ask. She was quite certain she would not be spending Christmas night with her husband.

Without speaking, Peter pulled Judy into his arms, making her feel safe and loved. The moment ended too soon when Peter whispered, "Angel, that was the Field Office. Something needs my attention right away."

"Is it about the man I saw?" asked Judy.

"You know I can't answer that question," Peter replied as he stroked her hair. "This assignment might take a few days so I probably won't be back tomorrow. I will call when I can. I told Horace about the man who resembles me and asked him to tell Honey and your parents. A car will pick me up soon, Angel. Will you walk me to the door?"

Judy handed Peter his coat and scarf. She watched him bundle up, and then, forgetting her own coat, followed him out onto the porch. A blast of icy wind made her shiver. It wasn't long before the FBI car pulled up and Peter reluctantly hurried down the porch steps.

Mrs. Bolton insisted that Judy spend the night, and she accepted without protest. She didn't relish driving back to her empty house in Dry Brook Hollow over dark, slippery roads. She'd have Blackberry for company, but even though he was a remarkable cat who had helped Judy solve mysteries, he wasn't Peter.

In her old bedroom, Judy had a hard time falling asleep. She knew that a good FBI wife should be content to leave such mysteries unsolved, but Judy never could ignore a puzzling situation, especially one so personal. She knew from experience that a mystery would nag her until she was forced to investigate.

But Judy also knew that becoming involved in Peter's cases could cause problems. She remembered the time she had followed Peter to a house where the FBI had a shoot-out. Later, Peter said that if he had known Judy was in the bullet's path, he would have allowed the criminal to escape rather than fire his gun.

"This time will be different. I won't meddle in Peter's business," Judy resolved before she finally pulled the quilts over her head. She ordered herself not to ponder the mystery any longer and managed to drift off sometime after midnight.

CHAPTER VI

A Trip to Bradford

THE day after Christmas was bitterly cold, and ominous gray clouds forecast snow. Honey called midmorning.

"Will you drive to Bradford with me right away? Before we went to bed last night, Grandpa said that snow was in the forecast for this evening. If we go now, we should be able to miss it. The roads might be bad tomorrow."

"How soon do you want to leave?" asked Judy.

"I can be ready in half an hour."

Judy hadn't planned to stay overnight in Farringdon, but fortunately the corduroy slacks and soft sweater her parents had given her for Christmas were perfect for this cold day. As she observed her reflection in the mirror, she noticed the frozen tear necklace in its velvet box. Blackberry noticed it too and sprang to the top of Judy's dresser, batting the diamond with his paw. "Miiaow!"

Judy dangled the gem just out of reach. Blackberry batted it again. His head darted from side to side, watching the movement of the shiny object. To Judy it seemed as if her cat were smiling happily.

"You're right, Blackberry," she told her pet. "This is a beautiful necklace, and I should enjoy wearing it." Judy fastened the clasp and hurried downstairs.

She welcomed the diversion of the trip. Looking for Mike should keep Judy's mind off Peter's assignment. Snowflakes spattered against the windshield by the time the girls were halfway to Bradford. Undaunted, Honey turned on the wipers. Judy had confidence in her sister-in-law's driving. Honey's skills had increased after negotiating the winding roads on their long trip to Yellowstone last spring.

"I loved yesterday," said Honey. "My grandparents kept talking about what a wonderful Christmas Day it was. And everyone was fascinated with the story of the Frozen Tears."

Judy fingered the diamond pendant that sparkled against her sweater and remembered Peter's sweet words.

"Horace picked out a thoughtful present for you, too," said Judy.

"Yes, he did," smiled Honey.

Judy couldn't resist adding, "Maybe next year he will give you a diamond." After all, Horace had said he didn't mind Judy and Honey talking about the relationship.

"I don't think so," said Honey.

"Why not?"

"He gave me one this year."

Judy turned and stared at Honey in astonishment. "Horace gave you a diamond?" Judy asked incredulously. Immediately her eyes traveled to Honey's left hand, covered by driving gloves.

"Not a diamond ring," laughed Honey when she saw where Judy's eyes were resting.

"Horace gave you a diamond but not a ring?" Judy was genuinely confused.

"He gave me a necklace," said Honey.

"A Frozen Tear necklace?" asked Judy. That seemed like too much of a coincidence.

"No, a necklace from Lawrence Jewelers. I'll show it to you when we stop. I'm wearing the necklace under my turtleneck. I didn't want people to ask about it."

"I don't understand." Judy was bewildered. Why would Honey want to conceal a present from Horace?

"I'm sure Horace won't mind me telling you

about the necklace. It should be obvious that he wants to marry me. He certainly isn't secretive about it. Remember when he and Peter were playing chess and Horace announced that I could have half his ivory chess set if I married him? I know it seems like he is joking when he makes such comments, but he's serious. I think he wants to keep reminding me of his intentions without really proposing. Also, he doesn't want a marriage proposal to be refused, so it's his way of feeling me out to see where I stand."

Judy did know that Horace was serious about Honey. He might take Holly Potter, Judy's neighbor, to square dances, but his heart seemed to stay with Honey. Honey's heart was the one that wavered. She alternately dated Forrest Dean, her boss's son, and Horace, and although Honey wasn't consistent about her preference, she was consistent with her jealousy of the girls who received Horace's attention.

"Sometimes I thought I loved Horace and wanted to marry him, and then other times I thought I didn't. I was afraid I would lose him while I made up my mind," explained Honey. "I finally realized that the problem was not whether or not I wanted to marry Horace, but when. I realized I loved him, but I just wasn't ready for marriage."

"We're the same age and I've been married two years," Judy reminded her.

"We're different. I needed time to catch up with those of you who had a normal childhood. Remember, I had two mothers. One didn't raise me right, and the other died before she could raise me at all. That makes a big difference."

Judy understood that her friend's situation was unusual.

"I have to consider my grandparents as well," Honey continued. The day will come when they can't live by themselves. Horace recently told me that he wants to build a house that will accommodate their needs as well as ours. Since the land he inherited is across the road from your farmhouse, Grandma and Grandpa will be close to both their grandchildren. Judy, I don't think you know what a treasure your brother is."

"I do when Horace helps me in a crisis or I am scared of losing him. When he was trapped under the fountain at the Brandt estate, I thought I couldn't stand it if something happened to him," Judy admitted.

"I decided I was ready for marriage and gave some hints to Horace. I expected he might give me a ring for Christmas. When Mike's letter was returned, I couldn't think of anything but my missing brother. Not knowing where he was made me realize that, right now, I've got more important things to worry about than romance."

"I know you miss Mike," Judy said quietly. "You must be worried sick about him."

"I am. I have to find him, but it's more than that. I am not sure how to explain."

"Don't feel like you have to explain, but I am curious about the diamond," said Judy.

"I didn't want to disappoint Horace or hurt his feelings, and yet I knew I wasn't really ready to marry him. The solution became clear when we were standing in line at the bakery on Christmas Eve. I heard a high school boy telling his friend that he was giving his girlfriend a pre-engagement ring. It may seem silly for kids to do that, but I decided that Horace and I needed to be pre-engaged. We could make a private commitment to each other that one day we will be married but not an engagement that was public. As soon as I had a solution to my problem, a weight slipped off my shoulders. An official engagement brings so much pressure, and I'm just not ready to make wedding plans."

"I know exactly what you mean," Judy assured her. "The moment Peter and I announced our engagement, the questions began. The hardest one was 'Where are you going to live?' I didn't have an answer for six months, not until my grandmother's will was read. Does Horace understand how you feel and why you aren't ready to become engaged?" asked Judy.

"He called after I got home from shopping on Christmas Eve, and I asked him to come over as soon as he could. It would be awkward if Horace proposed and I turned him down, and I might not have had the courage to refuse if he were holding the ring in his hand. We had a serious talk about our relationship. I told him I couldn't marry him, or even promise to wear a ring, until I made peace with my past. Horace understood and agreed."

"So the diamond necklace is a substitute for a diamond ring?" asked Judy.

"Isn't it a wonderful idea! Horace immediately went to Mr. Lawrence and asked him to reset the diamond from the ring he was planning to give me. Of course, Mr. Lawrence was too busy to fix it Christmas Eve, but he rushed and did it yesterday after Christmas dinner. He must think a lot of Horace. I had no idea what Horace had in mind when he called and insisted on taking me to breakfast this morning. He's never done that before, but he wanted me to have the necklace right away. Once we make an official announcement, Horace will have the diamond put back into the ring."

"Are you going to keep the necklace hidden until then?" asked Judy.

"Probably not. I'm just not ready for people to ask if it is a Christmas present and who gave it to me. I don't mind people knowing I love Horace. When we stop the car, I'll show the necklace to you and wear it for the world to see. There isn't anyone in Bradford who would care about my diamond."

Honey's confidences ended because the girls

were heading into what promised to be a storm, and driving required her full attention. Thankfully, Bradford was not much farther. The quest for Mike Vincenzo would be a good old-fashioned adventure. As they drove north, the snow became denser and the flakes larger. Fields along the road, filled with crops in warmer weather, were unbroken stretches of white. Occasionally a mailbox on a post jutted out of the snow, but those boxes were few and far between. They passed several barns, their weathered gray boards blending into the winter landscape.

"If I had some red paint," Honey declared, "I'd splash it onto those dreary barns."

"That would certainly brighten up the landscape," Judy agreed.

"I should have driven to Bradford the day the letter was returned," Honey said. "We could have avoided this snowstorm."

Thankfully, the snow had lessened considerably by the time Honey reached the small village of Bradford. In seconds, they had passed the main section of town and turned right on a narrow side road.

"There's the Smolletts' mailbox," Honey said. "We're about to solve the mystery of Mike's disappearance."

But they had only gone a few feet along the snow-covered drive when Honey stopped abruptly. In a soft voice she said, "We're not going to find Mike in there. At least, I hope we aren't."

Where a house once stood, the girls saw only charred timbers poking splintered ends through the snow. Fire had destroyed the Smollett home.

"Let's question the neighbors," Judy suggested.

Honey backed her car down the driveway and stopped in front of the closest farmhouse. At first glance, the place didn't look promising. Then Judy noticed a white cat with yellow eyes staring at them from the window.

When they rang the bell, a large man with a gray beard answered the door. He cradled a black cat that reminded Judy of Blackberry.

"We're looking for Mike Vincenzo who was living on the Smollett farm," said Honey anxiously. "We didn't know there had been a fire…"

The man immediately invited them inside. "Call me Bill," he said, moving a gray tabby aside to make room for Judy on the couch. Honey sat in a nearby armchair and explained their mission.

Bill smiled. "Sure, I know Mike. He lent me a hand with the chores, and I sure miss his help."

"Was Mike hurt in the fire?" Honey asked, voicing her greatest fear.

"Mike's fine. The way I heard the story, Ethel Smollett left a candle burning the night the power was knocked out. Sam and Mike were away that night, and she got burned pretty badly," Bill explained. "She was in the hospital in Buffalo, but now she's recovering at her sister's house, which is near a rehabilitation center. Sam moved up there and plans to stay until she's better. He said he didn't know when they would be back, if ever. Mike needed to find another job and said he was going to head for New York. He said some men from his old neighborhood might help him find work."

"Thank you so much for the information," said Honey. "If you happen to hear from Mike, would you please let me know?" She pulled a sheet from the small sketchpad she always kept in her purse and wrote her name, address, and phone number.

As they stepped off the porch, Honey said, "I'm so relieved!"

"What's next?" asked Judy as they climbed back in Honey's car. She hoped Honey didn't plan on driving straight to New York City.

Honey didn't reply until they were back on the main road. "I guess I learned everything I can in Bradford. Let's go home before the snow returns. Knowing that Mike is in the old neighborhood makes him as good as found. I know several neighbors who would help him. I bet I can find Mike in a day or two."

Honey's words were punctuated by a loud thump as something collided with her windshield. At the same time, the car's back wheels skidded. Honey steered the car out of the skid and headed back in the right direction just as another white ball hit the glass on the passenger side. It was fol-

lowed by an onslaught of large, pounding hail-
stones.

"We should stop somewhere until this hail-
storm passes," Honey shouted over the sound.

"Where?" Judy called back. "If we keep moving, we might outrun the storm."

"Or drive farther into it," said Honey. "Didn't
we pass a railway trestle on the way here? We
might be safe under there."

"Yes, we did," said Judy.

They went around another bend and there it
was, looming in the distance. "We can park under
it," said Honey.

When they reached the railroad bridge, Honey pulled as far to the right as possible and put on
her hazard lights. Now that the car was no longer being battered by ice, they could talk without
shouting.

"Let's plan our trip to New York while we
wait," suggested Honey.

"I can't promise a trip to New York until I
talk to Peter."

"Whether or not you go, I want to leave as
soon as possible," said Honey.

A sudden rapping on Honey's window interrupted them. A man in a gray trench coat tapped
on the glass. He had sandy blond hair, and a black
muffler covered most of his chin.

CHAPTER VII

The Brass Kettle

"It's Peter!" Honey exclaimed and started to roll down her window until Judy grabbed her arm.

"Be careful. This man may not be Peter but a criminal who resembles him."

"A criminal?" Honey responded in surprise. "He looks like Peter, and why else would he stop to help us?"

"Roxy and I look alike," reminded Judy. "Please trust me, Honey."

"Do you want me to ignore him?" asked Honey. "I'm sure it's Peter."

"Go ahead and roll down your window. Just be careful, and don't say anything that you wouldn't say to a stranger," Judy cautioned.

"Hi," said Honey to the man outside their car.

"I saw your hazard lights blinking and wondered if you ladies needed help."

The man's voice was like Peter's. Still, Judy felt uncertain.

"We are waiting out the storm," said Honey.

"If you stay here, another car could skid into you," the man warned.

"I hadn't thought of that," replied Honey.

The longer the man stood there, the more nervous Judy felt. She had the feeling he was sizing them up.

"I'd love to continue this conversation, but I'm freezing out here," the man said. "A few miles up the road there's a small café called the Brass Kettle. It's a safer place to wait out the storm, and you can follow me there."

"We'll do that," Honey said cheerfully as she rolled her window back up and turned to Judy. "I guess Peter figures we'll talk when we stop at the restaurant."

Judy looked back. An unfamiliar red car was parked behind Honey's.

"Honey," she said. "That man isn't Peter. I think he's the shoplifter from Brandt's."

"What shoplifter?" asked Honey. Judy had forgotten that Honey had not heard the story.

"Do you remember when we thought we saw Peter at Brandt's jewelry counter?" asked Judy. "Well, the man in Brandt's wasn't Peter."

"It sure looked like Peter, and you opened the necklace on Christmas Day," Honey said.

"Yes, but remember Helen's letter. It was dated December 20th, so Peter bought my present before Christmas Eve," said Judy. "There's more. After the person I thought was Peter left the store, I noticed that the necklaces he had been looking at were gone. I knew they had been stolen when we saw the policemen and Mr. Brandt at the jewelry counter."

"Oh, Judy!" exclaimed Honey. "Why didn't you say something?"

"I didn't know what to say. Eventually I remembered that Peter said he was watching a man who had a 'slight resemblance' to him. I figured the shoplifting incident involved one of Peter's assignments. I told Peter what I saw, and he assured me that it wasn't him."

"What makes you think we just spoke with the shoplifter?" asked Honey. "He sounded like Peter."

"Roxy and I sound alike. My reason may seem silly, but this man used the term 'ladies' in a matter-of-fact manner, the way someone would address strangers. If the man were Peter, he would have used the word 'ladies' teasingly."

"It seems like a flimsy reason to doubt someone, but you're usually right," said Honey.

"My second reason may seem even sillier. If he was Peter, I would have felt comfortable being near him, but I wasn't," said Judy. "That's all the proof I really need."

"But you were fooled at Brandt's," said Honey.

"That situation was different," Judy explained. "I saw him from a distance and didn't talk with him."

"You're right. I know Horace by his heart, not by his looks. If he's not Peter, he might be dangerous. Should I go another way?"

Judy considered Honey's suggestion. She wasn't as unnerved as she had been when the man was standing beside Honey's window. If they ran from him, they would never discover his identity. However, would it be safe to follow him? Peter had said the shoplifter was not known to be violent. While she wavered, the red car turned down a side street and spared Judy from making a decision.

"I guess he changed his mind about lunch," said Judy.

"I see the Brass Kettle sign ahead, right next to the Second Chance Pawn Shop," said Honey. "He's gone and I'm hungry, so let's stop."

After they were seated at a table for four, Honey rearranged her necklace so it rested against her lavender turtleneck.

"It's lovely," Judy said warmly.

"Yes, it is," smiled Honey. "Horace chose the stone himself, although we discussed diamonds one day when we were window shopping. I would have been hesitant to choose one so exquisite."

"I am not going to hesitate about choosing something exquisite for lunch," said Judy. "I'm famished."

"Turn around and look at the people waiting for tables," said Honey after she had put down her menu. "Our man must have decided he wanted lunch after all."

When Judy turned, she saw the back of the man they had encountered under the bridge. The man didn't look as much like Peter as he had at Brandt's, but Judy couldn't pinpoint the exact difference. Was it the way he was standing? His sandy blond hair was the same style and color as Peter's. Even his height and build matched her husband's. If only he would turn so Judy could see his face. Judy studied the man as long as she dared. By now Judy was certain that the man wasn't her husband.

The café filled up quickly, and the line waiting for tables doubled in minutes. Judy occasionally peeked at the mystery man. When the waitress came to take their orders, she asked if they would share their table. "We are swamped because of the storm, and it will help us serve as many as possible. I'll find two nice ladies for you," she promised.

Judy turned and saw that the mystery man was the next customer waiting. Impulsively she said, "We don't mind an extra person. The next customer in line can sit with us."

Honey, who had a clear view of the waiting area, looked at Judy in amazement. "Are you sure you want to invite the...umm...UnPeter to join us?" she asked as soon as the waitress had left.

"I'm not looking for trouble, just complying with the waitress's request," smiled Judy. She leaned closer to whisper, "Let's try to get as much information as we can so we can help Peter."

Honey shivered. "I thought I was taking a risk when I decided to drive to Bradford with a forecast of snow later in the day. Little did I know my adventure would pale in comparison to the plan you just proposed...having lunch with a criminal who looks like my brother. I hope you know what you're doing."

Judy didn't have time to retract her offer because the hostess immediately seated the man and handed him a menu.

"I'm glad you made it here safely," their new lunch partner said. "How kind of you to share your table with me." From the corner of her eye, Judy observed the man as he read the menu.

She was right about this man not being Peter! The similarity to her husband was startling from a distance, but up close, the differences were obvious. His nose started out like Peter's, but the end of it was more slender, slightly more tapered. His lips were thinner. Where Peter's jaw was square and sturdy, this man's chin was more delicate, almost pointed.

In fact, the only physical similarities between Peter and this man were their height, their blue eyes and their hair. But perhaps it was more than that. When their lunch companion rubbed his hand through his thatch of sandy hair, the gesture was so like Peter's that Judy had to look away.

But was Honey also right? Had Judy's impulsiveness put them both in danger?

CHAPTER VIII

A Revealing Conversation

JUDY wasn't sure about the etiquette for sharing a table. Should she introduce herself and converse? If so, should she give her real name? This man might be playing the same game as Peter. The man Honey had dubbed "the UnPeter" might be watching the FBI agent and hoping for a chance to take his place. Judy decided that she would chat innocently with Honey. It would seem unusual for two friends to sit in silence.

Honey must have thought the same thing, for she asked, "Do you think Blackberry will be fine if it is snowing in Dry Brook Hollow? I guess there are plenty of mice for him to catch in the woods behind the house, and he can take shelter in the barn."

Good for Honey. Blackberry was a safe topic. "He's still with my parents, but even if he weren't, he knows how to take care of himself," said Judy.

"I remember now. Once he was missing for days. You and Peter saw his tracks end abruptly in the snow and were worried that a hawk had caught him."

Judy wished Honey had not mentioned Peter's name. Judy glanced again at their table partner. Maybe he hadn't heard what Honey said. Before Judy could respond, the waitress returned with their salads and steaming bowls of soup.

The man was paying some attention to them. He looked over at the girls' food before saying, "Soup and salad look good, but I think I prefer a steak sandwich."

"Sure. Anything else?" asked the waitress.

"Just coffee, please."

Sipping soup gave Judy an excuse not to talk. Honey was the one on the hot seat because she sat across from the familiar-looking stranger. Even though Judy suspected him of a crime, she found it hard to think of him as a shoplifter when his mannerisms were similar to Peter's.

"That's a beautiful necklace you're wearing," said the UnPeter.

At first, Judy thought he was talking to her and fingered her Frozen Tear. She wanted to ask him if he recognized it but didn't dare. Then she realized he was talking to Honey when he added,

"Marquise diamonds look modern to me, but they have been around for over two hundred years."

"Really? I didn't know that," said Honey. "The princess cut is fairly new, but the marquise seems more contemporary to me. Maybe it's because I hadn't seen marquise diamonds until recently. Most women wear the brilliant round."

"I didn't know you knew so much about diamonds," said Judy.

"I don't. Horace is the one who researched diamonds."

"That's my brother for you," said Judy. She knew Horace would not make a diamond purchase lightly.

"So your brother is a diamond expert?" asked the man.

"I wouldn't necessarily say that," Judy replied. "He's more of a scholar than a diamond expert. Diamonds just happen to be his current interest." Judy smiled at Honey.

Judy wondered if this man were going to mention her necklace. She thought she had seen him glance at it. If so, what should she say? Why had she thought inviting him to the table would be a good idea? The way it was turning out, she and Honey were giving information, not obtaining it.

Thankfully, his next question was about Blackberry. "I take it Blackberry is your cat because he eats mice."

"Yes," said Judy. "I've had him for a long time."

"I prefer dogs myself."

"Do you have a dog?" asked Judy.

"Only when I was a kid. I travel too much to keep a pet now." He paused before he added, "I'm an investment counselor."

"Do you have a business card you can give us?" Honey asked.

Good idea, thought Judy.

"I'd be glad to help such lovely ladies." He put his hand into his coat pocket but came up empty. "I must have left them in my other jacket." Judy wondered if he really had left his business cards elsewhere or if he didn't want to hand them one.

As soon as his steak sandwich arrived, he turned his attention to it. Judy was frustrated because she hadn't obtained a single clue for Peter and might not have another opportunity. What she really needed to do was call the Field Office. Aloud she told Honey, "I just remembered a call I need to make."

She retrieved coins from her change purse, but as she left the table, a woman came out of the restroom and entered the phone booth. Another person joined the line to use the phone, and Judy realized she'd lost her chance. She put the coins back in her purse and returned to her seat.

"Changed your mind?" the man asked.

"It looks like the phone will be tied up for some time."

The following silence was awkward until Judy heard a familiar voice singing a Christmas song on the jukebox.

"Listen, Honey!" Judy exclaimed. "Irene told me she was going to record some holiday songs." Irene Lang had lived on upper Grove Street and worked at the local mill until she married mystery writer Dale Meredith. She had a "golden voice" and now sang on her own television series in New York.

"So you know the Golden Girl?" remarked a waitress who had overheard Judy's comment.

"She's an old friend," Honey answered.

They were definitely revealing too much information. Judy nudged Honey with her foot and cast a meaningful glance in her direction. Honey immediately found a more innocent topic.

"Horace's present was so thoughtful. It occupied Grandma and me for hours last night. We went to bed way too late. "

"Horace was pleased you liked his gift," said Judy.

"He knows me well," smiled Honey, looking down at her necklace. "The old masterpieces are a special love of mine." Discussing two of Honey's favorite art cards from the game kept them engaged until they finished eating.

Anxious to report to Peter, Judy said, "We need to go, Honey."

"You're right, Judy. It will be a long drive if

the roads aren't cleared. It's a good thing you're not going back to Dry Brook Hollow tonight."

"Ladies, you were most gracious to allow me to share your table and enjoy your company," their table partner said with a charming smile. Before they could object, the man summoned the waitress and opened his wallet to pay the entire bill.

Judy glanced at the wallet hoping for a clue to the man's identity. She managed to look away before he turned and wished both girls a safe ride home.

Honey and Judy both thanked the man for lunch and returned to the car.

"What do you think?" Honey asked when they were alone.

"We didn't learn much about him," Judy sighed. I caught a quick glimpse of his license when he opened his wallet, but I only had time to see Oil City as part of his address.

"That was quick thinking! You also learned that he drives a red car, likes dogs, and is an investment counselor."

"Information about the red car may not be helpful. When we walked by it just now, I noticed it had a rental decal. I don't think the fact he owned a dog will be useful either," Judy sighed. "We told him more than he told us."

"Knowing that he is from Oil City could help," Honey speculated. "Even if you didn't learn anything else, what he learned about you is insignificant. You have a cat named Blackberry."

"He learned more than that," said Judy. "He knows I have a husband named Peter and whatever else he picked up."

"I realized my mistake in mentioning Peter as soon as I saw the look on your face. However, Peter could be a brother or a neighbor. I didn't say he was your husband."

"True. I should make notes about our conversation so I can tell Peter as soon as I reach him."

Judy pulled out a pen and notepad from her purse. "Let's start in order. He knows I have a cat named Blackberry."

"And that he catches mice in the woods behind your house," laughed Honey.

"Actually, that's important. We let our criminal know I live in a rural area, away from other houses."

"Oh," said Honey. "I shouldn't have mentioned Dry Brook Hollow."

Judy worked on her list as she and Honey traveled toward Farringdon.

"I'll read my list, and you can tell me if I forgot something," Judy said finally.

"I have a cat named Blackberry. I live in Dry Brook Hollow in a house surrounded by woods. I have a barn. A barn would be helpful for storing stolen goods or hiding a car."

"You are letting your imagination get the better of you...and of me. I can't drive and be scared at the same time."

"We have good reason to be scared," acknowledged Judy before she continued reviewing her list. "I know someone named Peter." She paused. "As you said earlier, he might not think Peter is my husband unless he already knew that before meeting us. I wonder if he knows about Peter."

"You can't worry about that now," advised Honey. "At least we didn't tell him our names."

"You called me Judy when we left."

"Did I? I'm sorry," said Honey. "What else is on the list?"

"You own a marquise diamond necklace. I own a Frozen Tear necklace, although I don't know if he noticed it. What do you think?"

"Leave it on the list. I noticed him watching you while he ate. If you are listing what the man might have seen, add the double ruby ring. He was on your right side and the ring is on your right hand."

"Good idea." Judy made the notation before she continued reading. "I have a brother named Horace."

"Add that Horace researched diamonds," interrupted Honey.

Judy made that notation before declaring, "We know Irene, the Golden Girl. That finishes the list."

"What about my art game?" asked Honey.

"I wasn't sure what to write. That entire conversation is bothering me for some reason."

"Why? We talked about my favorite cards from the game. That's all."

"I know something's wrong, but I can't put my finger on it. Let's remember everything we said, and I'll write down what's important."

"First, I said that I loved Winslow Homer's seascape," began Honey.

"And that your grandmother said that the colors were too dreary for her taste," added Judy.

"And I told her the fishermen intrigued me and..."

"Wait," Judy interrupted. "We never said we were referring to a game! I just realized that a criminal who steals and can possibly find my house may think that my brother, the diamond expert, gave you some valuable works of art. At the time I thought that was an innocent topic, but now I see it could have been the most dangerous topic of all!"

CHAPTER IX

Worries

"How could the UnPeter find your farm-house?" asked Honey.

"Anyone in Farringdon can direct him to Dry Brook Hollow. Once there, he can ask for directions to Judy's house. He could drop Horace's and Blackberry's names, to prove he knows me.

"True. But wouldn't he look for Horace, the diamond expert, or me, the owner of a marquise diamond and valuable works of art, rather than you?"

"For all he knows, I live with Horace. People are always telling me I look too young to be married. He was sitting on my right side so he may not have noticed my wedding ring. Even if he did, if my brother is rich, shouldn't I be wealthy too?" reasoned Judy.

"What should we do?" asked Honey.

"Call Peter right now! Pull over when you see a place with a pay phone."

Around the next curve was a gas station that looked promising. Judy bounded out of the car as soon as it stopped. She did not return as quickly. "I was put on hold and finally left a message for Peter to call," she explained. "There's nothing else to do but wait."

"Then let's plan our trip to New York City," said Honey. We can take the bus and stay with Pauline Faulkner."

"Pauline might not want company during the holidays," said Judy.

"Didn't you receive her Christmas card?" asked Honey. "Her father is leaving for a medical conference today. She mentioned that she was lonely and to please come anytime. We can see Irene too."

"Cards from both Pauline and Irene arrived the day before Christmas Eve. I tossed them on the kitchen table to open with Peter at dinner, and then we ate at Joe's Diner. We've been so busy that I forgot about them until now."

Judy wondered if she should go to New York City with Honey. If only she knew if their thief would turn up in Dry Brook Hollow. Judy preferred to stay and watch her home, but if Peter weren't there, she would be less lonely with Honey in New York. She would enjoy visiting Dale and Irene and especially seeing their daughter, little Judy Irene. When she visited New York, Judy always received a warm welcome at Pauline's elegant home in Gramercy Park.

It was almost four o'clock when Honey turned her car onto lower Grove Street. Judy gazed out the car window at the Farringdon-Pett mansion with its fairy-tale turrets. Most of the graceful residence was concealed by a grove of pine trees and a tall barberry hedge all adorned with tiny white lights sparkling in the snow. After seeing the Smolletts' burned house and Bill's old place with its feline occupants, the elegant homes of Farringdon's wealthiest residents were especially impressive.

"It's hard to believe that only yesterday Peter and I drove this same street and admired the Christmas decorations," mused Judy. "So much has happened."

When Honey pulled into the Boltons' driveway, Judy invited her in, but Honey declined the invitation.

"Horace and I are getting together tonight, and I need time to get ready. I'll phone you in the morning."

"I've been away too long, and I'm worried about my house. I've decided to drive home as soon as I say hello to Mother and put our Christmas gifts in the Beetle."

Judy ended up leaving one gift at her parents' house. During her absence, Peter's toy train en-

gine had gained a track on which to run and a
depot at which to stop.

"Horace and Peter's grandfather met down-
town and picked out the new train pieces," Mrs.
Bolton explained. "The snow kept your father
from having many patients this afternoon, so
he helped put the track together. Why don't you
leave it here until we take down the tree?"

Judy agreed. "It will be one less thing for me
to pack, and everyone can enjoy it here."

"Will you stay for dinner? Horace is having
dinner with Honey, and after the Christmas excitement, the house is too quiet."

"I want to be home before dark," said Judy.

Mrs. Bolton glanced out the window. "Even
if you leave as soon as you pack the car, it will be
dark before you arrive home. We can eat an early
supper. I am heating up Christmas leftovers, so
I will have supper ready as soon as your father
returns from a hospital call."

Judy agreed. Although she was impatient to
be back at the farmhouse, eating with her parents
was better than cooking a lonely meal.

Her father returned before Mrs. Bolton had
dinner on the table, and he brought a request
with him. "Today a salesman gave me some
samples of the medication I've recommended for
the young Piper boy. I know Roulsville is out of
your way, but would you mind taking them to the
Pipers? I'm concerned that the family may delay

buying this medicine at the store because of the expense."

Judy did mind because she would have to pass her home to reach Roulsville and then drive back. Although she loved the Piper children, it would delay her, especially today when she was worried about a possible robbery. Nevertheless, Judy couldn't refuse to help her friends. And her father. If she refused, she knew that he would make the trip himself.

As soon as the meal was over, Judy loaded the Beetle and departed, with Blackberry resting on the seat beside her. Few cars were on the road, and Judy kept her eye out for the red rental car. She knew any potential danger was her fault. If only she hadn't offered to share their lunch table. If only Honey hadn't mentioned Dry Brook Hollow. If only she and Honey hadn't talked so freely during the meal. If all the "if onlys" could be erased, there wouldn't be a way for Judy to be located. Or Peter. Did the suspect know he resembled an FBI agent? If so, how much danger was Peter facing?

At the Pipers, Judy enjoyed seeing the children's Christmas presents, but she was relieved when she said goodbye and started home.

New snow was falling and covering the tracks made earlier in the day. The sight of tranquil snowy fields usually soothed Judy. Tonight, the untainted snow seemed barren, almost ghostly.

The trees and their shadows against the whiteness of the snow exaggerated the darkness of the woods. Judy felt that something ominous awaited her.

Around the next bend loomed three broken pieces of concrete, illuminated by the moonlight reflecting off the snow-covered ground. They were the remains of the Roulsville dam. Judy had passed the grim reminder so often that she thought she had grown immune to its effect. Tonight, the memory was fresh. After she had won the Roulsville Spelling Bee, Arthur had driven her home and stopped his car by the dam. In the moonlight, he had pointed out the dam's cracks and said they could split wide open with the next heavy rain. Within twenty-four hours his prediction came true. Floodwaters destroyed Roulsville, including Judy's childhood home.

Judy wondered why the dam cast its gloom on her that evening. Was it because tonight's moonlight made the memorial of that fateful day more prominent? Or was it because it reminded her that sometimes things we dread do come true? Judy's impatience to be in Dry Brook Hollow turned into trepidation. Was it safe? The closer the Beetle came to its home, the more it lived up to its name and crawled.

"I'll stop at the Potters first and ask about their Christmas Day," Judy decided. Holly Potter, Judy's friend and nearest neighbor, lived with her sister Ruth and brother-in-law Eric.

If I am still nervous after our visit, I'll ask Eric to accompany me home, Judy decided while she waited on the doorstep with Blackberry in her arms.

Eric opened the door. "I'm surprised to see you," he greeted her. "This is a perfect evening for you and Peter to sit by your fireplace."

"Peter's away on an assignment. I stopped in because I was lonely," Judy confessed.

"It must be serious for him to leave in such bad weather."

"It was serious enough for Peter to leave last night," said Judy. "He's been gone since then which is the real reason I stopped by. I wasn't ready to face an empty house after spending yesterday and today with family."

"Then you'll be glad to know he's home so he can rest. Holly mentioned that he was sniffling."

"Sniffling?" Judy repeated with concern in her voice. "He didn't expect to be home so soon. Are you sure it was Peter?"

"As sure as I'm standing here," laughed Eric. "Ask Holly. When she saw the lights inside your house, she took over some Christmas cookies. She meant to deliver them the day before Christmas but couldn't catch anyone at home."

"We were in Farringdon," said Judy. If Holly had only seen Peter from a distance, Judy might be suspicious about the identification. However,

Holly knew Peter well and had seen him in a lighted house.

"Thanks for the information. I won't keep Peter waiting. I'll visit another time."

Judy made her way back to her car and drove to the farmhouse with a lighter heart. "Honey was right. I did let my imagination run away with me," she scolded herself. She and Peter could spend the evening sitting in front of the fireplace and enjoying the Christmas tree. More importantly, they could discuss the list she had made. With Judy's new information, perhaps Peter would be authorized to divulge more facts about his case.

Judy's plans evaporated as soon as she saw the farmhouse. Not a single light was shining, not even the porch light. Had Peter stopped for fresh clothes or a file from his office safe and left as quickly as he came? It was hard for Judy to have her hopes dashed so quickly. She dreaded entering the empty house after anticipating a reunion with her husband. She remembered Grandma Smeed quoting the proverb, "Hope deferred maketh the heart sick." If Judy thought her heart was sick after seeing a dark house, it was sicker when the door swung open before she could insert her key. Was the lock broken? Peter wouldn't have left the front door unsecured. Had her fears come true? Had the UnPeter paid the farmhouse a visit after Peter left? Was he still here, waiting in the dark house?

CHAPTER X

Robbed!

SEVERAL times in the past, Judy had thought someone might be in the farmhouse, and she had not been frightened. The first time was right after her honeymoon. Judy had felt the presence of someone in the cellar when she was looking for canned fruit and later heard noises. It turned out that Roberta, Judy's flower girl who later lived with Judy and Peter, was hiding in the cellar.

Several months later while Peter was away, Judy had heard footsteps during the night. Judy had convinced herself that nothing had happened, but someone had entered the farmhouse that night and stolen the portrait hanging over the fireplace. The last time Judy had heard noises and investigated, a 10-year-old boy was hiding in her attic.

This time, Judy's first reaction was to escape, not investigate, and she knew why she was so frightened. Instead of vague feelings, she had the unpleasant certainty that she had practically invited a charming stranger to rob her house! If Peter was hurt, Judy knew she would gain more by bringing help than by going inside.

Blackberry seemed to share his mistress's misgivings, as he stayed by Judy's ankles instead of darting into the house. Judy scooped him up, dashed to the Beetle and started the engine. Despite her haste, driving fast on the bumpy dirt road was not an option. Judy viewed each rut and patch of snow as an obstacle to quickly reaching the Potter home. The bright moon that had made the dam remnants eerie had slipped behind dark clouds, the light deserting Judy at a time when she would welcome its help.

Judy wasn't sure how long it took to reach her neighbors. She only knew it was too long before she reached the safety of the Potter house. Eric phoned the Roulsville police as soon as he heard Judy's breathless explanation.

"Oh, Blackberry, what have I done!" Judy sighed while waiting for the officers to arrive. If only she were in Farringdon, she could confide in Chief Kelly, whom she trusted completely. But she couldn't be in Chief Kelly's jurisdiction any more than she could change her other "if onlys."

A Roulsville police officer arrived at the Potter's home within minutes and reported that two others had gone directly to the Dobbs's house. Peter had worked with the Roulsville police in the past, so they knew he was an FBI agent. Was that why three officers had been sent?

"Exactly when did you leave your house and exactly when did you return?" asked the officer.

"I left Christmas morning and returned about 15 minutes ago," Judy replied.

"I wouldn't be surprised if there was a break-in on Christmas Day. Crooks know people are away, and the neighbors are too busy to notice unusual activity."

"Whatever happened occurred within the last couple of hours," Judy stated with conviction.

The young officer seemed surprised. "Do you have facts to back that statement?"

"No," Judy admitted. Suspicions about a lunch conversation were not facts. Even if she had facts, she should tell them to Peter first.

"Yes, you do have facts," countered Holly. "I saw Peter before dinner. When I saw the lights in the house, I took him some cookies. If the house had been robbed, he would have mentioned it or called the police himself."

"Miss Potter, did Mr. Dobbs indicate that anything was abnormal?"

"No, he just thanked me," Holly answered.

"What time did you see Mr. Dobbs?"

"A little after five o'clock," Holly replied. "I

know because my nephew's favorite TV program had just finished. He watches it while my sister fixes dinner."

The officer turned to Judy. "Do you have any valuables that could be easily pawned? Jewelry, guns, coin collections, antiques?" From the way the officer rattled off his list, Judy knew the question was routine.

"I am wearing the only jewelry that has any value, but I do have some antiques in the kitchen."

"I'll give my partners that information. Stay here until we let you know it's safe. Hopefully it is just a rickety old door blown open by today's storm."

"But Peter was home after the storm ended," insisted Holly.

"Yes, and our door isn't rickety. It's fairly new," added Judy. She and Peter had replaced it at the same time a picture window had replaced the "everyday door" in the kitchen.

"All the more reason for you to stay here while we check," said the police officer.

The longer it took the officers to return, the more Judy prepared herself for the worst. She didn't care if her entire house had been emptied as long as her husband was safe.

A different police officer returned to accompany Judy to the farmhouse. "You can leave your car here and ride over with me." He presented it as an option, but from the way it was said, Judy knew it was a command.

"So someone was in the house?" asked Judy.

"It appears so."

"Do you want me to go with you?" asked Eric.

Judy would have liked company, but she didn't want Eric to hear any confidential information she might feel compelled to reveal.

"I'll be fine," Judy assured him as she and Blackberry followed the officer to the door. "You have already been good neighbors tonight, and I'll be back later for the car."

"If you don't feel like coming out again, I'll drive your car over."

"Thanks, Eric." Judy kept a spare car key at the Potters' house.

In the police car, the officer said, "It appears that someone did enter the house. We searched and no one is there now. We need you to inspect everything and tell us what is missing."

Judy's primary concern was Peter, not possessions. "Did it look like someone had been hurt?" she asked.

"There weren't any bloodstains or signs of a scuffle, if that's what you mean," was his matter-of-fact response. "The robbery must have occurred after your husband left."

Judy sighed with relief. Nothing else mattered. Grandma Smeed had left Judy items that had been in the family for well over a hundred years. If her grandmother's Wedgwood and milk glass china had been stolen, Judy would miss the link they gave her to her ancestors and the beauty they brought to her kitchen, but Peter's safety was what mattered.

Judy was still preparing herself for what she would find when the farmhouse came into view. Her home blazed with lights that could be seen through the bare trees. Light even shone from the windows on the third floor where Grandma Smeed's sewing machine and old calendars were kept.

Blackberry sprung from his mistress's arms as soon as the door of the police car was opened. Judy didn't know what she expected to see, but the living room appeared normal. If it hadn't been for the police presence, she would have thought the evening's events had been a dream. However, as soon as she stepped into the kitchen, Judy knew the house had been robbed. The shelves of the corner hutch that held the Wedgwood pieces were empty. The cabinet door below was flung open, and her grandmother's dolls were gone. Although the cabinet occupied a small corner, its emptiness made the entire kitchen seem bare.

"Tell me what's missing, and I'll make an itemized list," said the officer.

"I'll try to remember." Judy wasn't sure she could recall each item. The Wedgwood pieces were rarely used. She started with her favorite, the strawberry plate, so named because it was made to look like a basket of strawberries. When Judy was sick as a child, Grandma Smeed had served Judy strawberries and whipped cream from the dish. It was the only time Judy could recall that piece being used.

The memory brought tears to Judy's eyes. As much as Judy thought she had steeled herself against possible loss, she hadn't. Peter might call her "Angel" at times, but Judy was a human girl with a tender heart, and she immediately missed her grandmother's treasures. Money couldn't replace the precious items and the memories they held.

"Next item," said the officer. Judy wondered how long he had been waiting for her to continue.

Judy surprised herself by recalling each piece. If the police recover Grandma's dishes, I am going to use them, she resolved. It's better for them to be lost through breakage than not used at all.

It was harder to remember the details of the rare dolls kept in the bottom cabinet of the china closet. That would change, too. If Peter made a shelf, Judy could display them in the spare bedroom. She would have to dust them, a task she despised, but the inconvenience would be worth it.

After the kitchen was examined, the police insisted that Judy check the living room even though it looked untouched. It seemed a waste of time to her, but the officer was right. The milk glass hen that sat on her bookshelf was missing.

"Another antique. There's the pattern," said the officer who had driven Judy home. "Has anyone appraised your possessions recently or offered to purchase them? There are crooks who pose as appraisers."

"No. I didn't have a reason to have them appraised, but I know there are crooked appraisers."

"That's right, you helped break up one of those scams," remembered the officer. Judy had helped catch a man who posed as an antique appraiser in order to case the homes of wealthy people. Later he would return and steal the items he had appraised.

This could be a routine holiday break-in by someone who suspected the old-fashioned house contained antiques. Was the officer right? Judy wasn't sure if she was relieved or not. She would like to think her words at lunch had not caused the robbery.

"I'm sorry, could you repeat what you were saying?" asked Judy after she realized the youngest officer was speaking to her.

"I asked if you wanted to inventory this room next." The officer nodded toward Peter's office, which had once been a parlor bedroom.

Judy checked the door and, as expected, found it locked. "That's my husband's office. It has his law books and work papers. No antiques there." Even if the room had been burglarized, Peter kept confidential files in a safe.

"Are you satisfied that we have cataloged everything missing downstairs?"

"Yes," said Judy.

"Then let's proceed upstairs."

"I don't have antiques upstairs," Judy informed him.

"You never know what someone will take," laughed one of the officers. "The first robbery I investigated included the theft of a frozen pizza and drinks from the refrigerator."

One officer remained downstairs while the other two climbed the steps with Judy to the spare bedroom. Judy and Peter thought of it as Roberta's room, even though the little girl had been found and returned to her family two years earlier. The area looked intact at first glance. The dresser was empty, and the closet contained out-of-season clothes. Nothing seemed amiss until Judy's eyes swept the room a second time.

"Is something wrong?" asked one of the officers.

Judy realized that the Roulsville police had been doing more than taking notes of items. They had been gauging her reactions to the crime scene and had noticed her flinch.

Yes, something was terribly wrong, but the police would never understand. The thief had taken her wedding picture!

CHAPTER XI

A Change of Plans

"THIS bedroom is a guest room," Judy said, recovering her composure.

"And nothing is missing?" The officer nodded toward the bare dresser top.

"We keep out-of-season clothes in the closet. That's all," said Judy. Had she fooled them?

In Judy and Peter's bedroom, the wedding photos had been left behind. Judy was sure she knew why. Her jewelry box had been dumped out, and its contents were scattered across the bed, but nothing appeared to be missing.

Judy followed the police officers to the third floor. "This is a storage area," she told them.

"I'm surprised the sewing machine was left if our thief was after antiques," one of the officers remarked. "It looks valuable."

"I'm sure it is. It's dated 1890 and is in perfect condition," said Judy. "But if a man were working alone, he couldn't carry it out without help."

"Yes, but he could take the drawers. Those gargoyles are priceless," stated the other officer. The drawers of the sewing machine table were elaborately carved with grinning gargoyles holding the door pulls in their teeth.

"How do you know that?" his partner asked.

"My mother-in-law inherited a machine like this one, and she sure is proud of it."

"I guess that's all," said Judy and led them downstairs.

"You should be safe, even with a busted door knob. I don't think your robber has a reason to return."

"I may drive back to Farringdon and stay with my parents tonight. I haven't decided." Judy gave the men the Boltons' phone number so they could reach her there if necessary.

The officers finished their paperwork at the kitchen table, and then Judy reviewed the inventory of missing items to make sure it was correct.

Peter called as soon as the officers were in their cars. "Peter, you won't believe what happened today," Judy began. "I had so much to tell you when I called after lunch, and even more has happened. It's all my fault, and you would think by now that I would have learned my lesson..."

"Slow down, Sweetheart, and start at the beginning," Peter interrupted.

It was hard to start with the tap on Honey's car window, although Judy knew the break-in would make more sense if Peter had all the facts. Judy took a deep breath and started her story.

"I don't see how you can listen so patiently without wanting to know how it ended," Judy said when, once more, Peter had stopped her from digressing or jumping to the conclusion of her day.

"I've had practice. Remember, much of my job is routine questioning."

"I hope I am more than a job to you," Judy retorted. She knew she was being unfair.

Peter understood the meaning behind Judy's words. Instead of answering her accusation, he offered words of understanding. "I know it was hard to have me leave on Christmas Day and then face everything that happened today. I'm sorry I'm not there to help you now."

"I shouldn't have said what I did, and yes, it's been a hard day. What should I do next?"

"I won't know until you finish the story you were so impatient to tell me," Peter teased gently.

To expedite the story, Judy jumped from lunch to finding the door unlocked. She continued without being distracted until she came to the scene where she was describing the Wedgwood pieces to the police.

"Peter, would Grandma think I was careless?"

"You weren't careless, Angel. If anything, you were too careful because you never used the Wedgwood."

"I've been thinking that if Grandma's things are recovered, we are going to make sure we enjoy them."

"Absolutely, and you need to stop thinking of them as your grandmother's things. They belong to you."

"They belong to us. Remember when we built the shelves for your home office? I thought we could build a shelf in the spare bedroom. I could display the dolls there. One day our own little girl might enjoy them. Of course, I might never see Grandma's dolls again."

"Don't give up hope, and if nothing is found, there will be other treasures. I'll build you a display shelf the next free day I have," Peter promised.

"I still wonder if Grandma would be mad at me."

"I think you know the answer to that," said Peter.

"She would tell me not to cry over spilled milk."

"Your grandmother loved you, much more than any possessions."

Peter was so comforting.

"Yes," agreed Judy. "As much as she might

be disappointed, Grandma would be glad that no one was hurt, and that brings me to something else."

"The 'something else' is going to have to wait. I have just enough time to make another call before I report back. I'll try to phone again soon."

Peter hung up before Judy could tell him what was missing from Roberta's room.

"Well how do you like that?" Judy asked Blackberry. "I wonder who he had to call."

Judy received her answer when the phone rang. It was Horace.

"Hi, Sis. Peter called and asked me to run out to the farmhouse. I can either bring you back here or, if you want to sleep in your own bed tonight, I can pack a bag and stay. Which is it?"

"I don't know."

"Then I'll pack a bag, and you can make up your mind while I drive out. Either way I'll be prepared," said Horace.

"I thought you had a date with Honey."

"Stop avoiding the subject."

"I think you are the one avoiding the subject. Really, Horace, Blackberry can keep me company."

"I don't think Blackberry is the company Peter had in mind, and after what Honey told me about your adventures today, I agree with Peter. I'll be there soon." Horace hung up before Judy could respond.

Judy didn't want to leave her house vulnerable or miss an opportunity to catch the thief if he returned. However, when she went upstairs and saw the disarray on her bed, she knew that spending the night alone with the door unlocked was unwise. She resented both being frightened out of her own home and giving in to Horace, but she didn't think she had a choice.

No sooner had she put her overnight bag beside the door than she returned it to her room and exchanged it for a suitcase. She might as well stay on Grove Street until Peter came home. Better yet, she would go to New York City with Honey. Peter would be pleased to have her out of harm's way. Judy smiled when she thought how quickly Peter had called Horace.

It was too late to call a locksmith and have the lock replaced. Instead she called Red and asked him to replace the lock first thing in the morning and care for everything while she was away. Red had helped Judy's grandparents with the farm and had recently built a small house on the land he had inherited from them.

"I'll be glad to take care of the farm; don't you worry," Red reassured her. "Things won't get busy around here until springtime. Last season I could barely keep up with my landscaping business. That might seem like a good problem, but you lose customers if you can't deliver what you promise."

"Thanks, Red. I knew I could count on you. Please be sure to call the police if you see anything or anyone suspicious."

"Of course," Red assured her.

"I shouldn't be in New York City long. I wish there was some way I could repay you for all your help."

"Well, if you find a hard worker who is tired of city life and likes outdoor work, bring him back to me."

Judy's next call was to the Potters.

"I'll drive your car over," Eric promised. "It will make the house look occupied."

"Thanks for everything tonight," Judy replied, feeling grateful for her good neighbors.

"Oh, brother, someone did a job on the lock," Horace commented when he arrived. "Let me figure out a way to secure it before we leave. You don't want to come home with gifts from the squirrels awaiting you in the kitchen." His improvised latch wouldn't keep out a man, but it would protect the house from the elements.

"Do you plan to move in or did you pack bricks?" Horace teased when he lifted her suitcase into his convertible.

"Neither. Honey asked me to go to New York City with her, and I thought that would keep me out of trouble."

"So you admit you have a hard time staying out of trouble. What is it this time?"

"Didn't Honey tell you about our trip, especially lunch?" asked Judy.

"Yes, but we spent most of our time talking
about Mike and her planned trip to New York.
She received a letter from Mike today. "

"I'm surprised she didn't call me."

"I guess she didn't have time before our date,"
shrugged Horace. It seemed like a plausible reason to him.

Judy didn't think so. In the past, a date with
Horace would not have kept Honey from phon-
ing Judy with such exciting news. Judy knew that
her friendship with Honey changed when Judy
married Peter. Peter was the first one Judy turned
to with her joys as well as her sorrows. His adventures and interests took priority over those of her
friends, including Honey, who was her best friend
and Peter's sister. Given that Horace and Honey
were almost engaged, it shouldn't be surprising
that her best friend would talk with her future
husband before Judy. Still, Judy had mixed feelings about this turn of events.

"I don't like growing up," Judy complained.

"Wow, this is a red-letter day. You admit that
you get into trouble and now you admit that you
haven't finished growing up," teased Horace.

"I take that back. I don't like you and Honey
growing up." Judy knew she wasn't making sense.

Horace showed that he understood when he

answered, "I always thought you approved of our relationship."

"I do. I just don't like the relationship with my best friend changing," sighed Judy.

"It changed a long time ago. Are you just noticing it?" chided Horace. "When you married, not only did Honey's best friend move to another town, but so did a brother she loved. A double whammy."

"I hadn't thought about it from Honey's point of view," said Judy.

"No matter how much you care about Honey, you and Peter come first with each other. Don't begrudge Honey for having someone who puts her first and her returning the compliment."

"I guess I am self-centered. I wasn't fair to Peter either when he called tonight."

"No, you are not self-centered. In fact, I could be accused of being selfish by encouraging Honey's trip. The sooner she understands her childhood, the sooner we can marry. A trip to New York should speed up the process. The trip will also help you. The sooner I marry Honey, the sooner she will live across the street, closer than ever."

"That's true," agreed Judy.

That ended their conversation because Judy didn't want to discuss the robbery. She closed her eyes for a moment and didn't realize she had slept until Horace pulled into the driveway. Their mother, a coat thrown over her shoulders, was waiting on the porch. She called out before Horace parked the car.

"Peter's on the phone. I told him I heard your car," Mrs. Bolton said.

Judy shook herself awake as she hurried into the house and grabbed the receiver. She didn't wait to see who might overhear or give Peter a chance to speak.

"He knows he resembles you, Peter. I know he knows and he is planning to use it to his advantage. Otherwise he wouldn't have stolen our wedding photograph."

CHAPTER XII

A Trip to New York

"Is it the photograph of us with Roberta?" asked Peter.

"Yes, and he didn't steal the wedding photographs in our bedroom, the one of me by myself and the one of me with Pauline after she caught my bouquet. That means he wanted your picture, Peter."

"That is significant, Angel. It changes a lot of things. Were any of the photographs from our wedding album missing? If our suspect wanted to impersonate me, those photos would provide more information than the snapshot Roxy took."

"I didn't think to check," said Judy. "And Peter, I didn't mention it to the police."

"Good. I'll get a copy of the police report."

"Does the missing photo mean you are in danger? I mean more danger than usual?" asked Judy.

"It means I might be taken off the assignment, or maybe we'll have to make our move sooner than we expected. We don't want this man to discover he resembles an FBI agent and then use the information to his advantage."

"I should have mailed the photograph to Roberta like I planned, but I liked looking at it," said Judy. "It made the room seem less lonely."

"The new doll shelf will make the room seem less lonely. I have to go, Angel. I hate to cut our conversation short, but I need to report the missing photo."

"I am so sorry for messing up everything."

"You haven't messed up anything. The information about Oil City may help us. For some reason, Oil City rings a bell. And making our move sooner may turn out to be for the best. The FBI will probably send someone tonight to investigate. I might come myself. The only thing I want you to do is stay away from Dry Brook Hollow for the next few days."

"Honey is going to New York City, and tonight I decided I would go with her."

"Good plan. In fact, that gives me an idea. You could visit some of the antique shops and see if you spot any of your missing heirlooms. We suspect a local pawn shop of fencing stolen jewelry and antiques, and those items often find their way to New York City. I can't give you the details, of course, but I see no harm in your looking around."

"There was a pawn shop right next to the Brass Kettle in Bradshaw. Maybe that's why the man who looks like you was there," Judy said. "Oh, Peter, wouldn't it be wonderful if I found the antiques in New York!"

"It's a small chance, so don't get your hopes up. One other thing. If you do find any of our antiques, call the Field Office immediately and please let us handle it."

After Judy told Peter good-bye, she noticed that Horace was talking with her mother and father in the hallway. From the look on Mrs. Bolton's face, Judy figured Horace was telling them about the suspect who resembled Peter. Judy was glad she didn't have that unpleasant job.

The next day Judy could read the worry in her mother's face as she urged her to be careful in New York City.

Horace drove the girls to catch the early morning bus. As they arrived at the terminal, he handed Honey a carefully wrapped package.

"I'm so excited that you've finished your manuscript!" Honey said, giving Horace a smile. "I'm sure the agent will love it and want to represent you."

Honey had persuaded Horace to allow her to bring his manuscript to New York in hopes that literary agent Emily Grimshaw would agree to look it over. Horace had finally agreed to say it was finished. He had been working on his detective novel for years, basing it on Judy's sleuthing adventures, which he had been covering as a reporter for the *Herald*.

"Imagine—I'll be a famous author and we'll live in the lap of luxury!" Horace quipped. "Take good care of my manuscript, and yourselves too." Then in a more serious voice he added, "I admit that I'm worried and wish I didn't have to work. Maybe I can come later."

"I understand," Honey reassured him. "It won't be the same, but Judy is with me."

With mixed feelings, Judy left the couple and boarded the bus. It must have been a long good-bye because Judy was settled before her best friend started down the aisle.

Honey stored her carry-on bag in an overhead compartment and dropped into the seat next to Judy. She smiled gently before saying, "I just realized how insensitive I have been to you. Until I had to leave Horace this morning, I never understood what you went through whenever Peter was away on assignments."

Tears formed in Judy's eyes. "Oh, Honey, I am the one who has been insensitive. I didn't realize what it was like to be moved to second place."

On the ride out of Farringdon, the girls had a heartfelt talk. Afterward, Judy was ready for

time alone with her own thoughts. She was relieved when Honey took out a magazine and began thumbing through its pages. Judy wished she
could lose herself in a magazine, but she had real-
life concerns, a criminal posing as Peter. Judy was
frustrated that there was nothing she could do to
help. The long trip seemed even longer than usual, and the stops along the way seemed endless.

Pauline Faulkner met them at the bus terminal. Like Judy, Pauline was a doctor's daughter.
The girls had become friends when Dr. Faulkner,
a psychiatrist and neurosurgeon, had been instru-
mental in solving the mystery of Honey's identity.
Dr. Faulkner had matched Honey's thumbprint
with Baby Grace Thompson's print. The doctor
had kept the unusual thumbprint on file because
the center whorl formed the shape of a heart.

Pauline treated them to lox and bagels at a
Manhattan deli near the office where she worked
for Emily Grimshaw. More importantly, she treated them to the latest news of their New York
friends. Irene and Dale were drawing up plans to
remodel the Sand Castle, their vacation cottage
on Fire Island. Another friend, Sylvia Weiss, had
started college and was considering a career as an
art therapist.

"I guess art therapy will ensure a more stable
income than cutting silhouettes at parties," said
Honey. Sylvia had been cutting silhouettes when
Judy and Honey had met her over five years ago.

"I never knew how hard artists worked to support themselves until I met Sylvia," Pauline remarked.

"Even if my job at Dean Studios is stifling at times, I'm grateful I can earn money in the art field," said Honey.

Pauline expressed surprise. "I thought you loved your job."

"Most of the time I do, but I would like the freedom to pursue my own ideas, not just the ideas of a customer or boss," Honey explained.

"Maybe you'll have an opportunity to do so," smiled Pauline. "Any chance for a ring to match that diamond necklace you're wearing?"

The question did not surprise Judy. Although Pauline enjoyed her job, she considered it temporary until she found the right man to marry, preferably someone who would provide her with a luxurious life as well as love. Pauline had no hesitation about saying what was on her mind. However, Honey's candor was a surprise.

"Yes, Horace is willing for me to quit my job when we marry so I can pursue my own artistic interests. I'm just not ready for marriage."

"What's holding you back?" Pauline asked. "Horace might not wait around forever."

"Horace says he is willing to wait. I have some things I need to do first, which is one of my reasons for coming to New York. I want to visit my old neighborhood and check on the family I used to live with."

Pauline's face reflected her dismay. "Why would you want to visit that neighborhood? Just thinking about it gives me the shivers."

Pauline lived in a large stone house with a roof garden where she could look down on the lights of Manhattan. To help solve the mystery of Honey's identity, Pauline had traveled to one of the dingiest sections of Brooklyn. She had visited the Vincenzo household and posed as a saleswoman handing out free samples. Mrs. Vincenzo had readily given out the names of household members to obtain free toothpaste and toothbrushes.

"The neighborhood doesn't frighten me," said Honey. "Remember, I grew up there. The residents may be poor, but most of them are hard-working people."

"Still, who do you have left there?" asked Pauline.

Judy wondered the same thing and waited for Honey's answer.

"A family on the corner was always kind to Mike and me, although they didn't care for the older Vincenzo boys, who were the neighborhood bullies. The woman across the street also looked out for us. And I never said good-bye to the woman who raised me. Mike and I just disappeared. Who knows what her sons told her. She might not have been the best mother, but for some reason she wanted me. I owe her something."

Judy had to disagree with Honey's charity toward the woman she had considered her mother for sixteen years. If Mrs. Vincenzo had not kept the child and pretended the little girl was her own, Honey and Peter would have been raised together.

Judy could tell from Pauline's expression that she also disagreed with Honey. Pauline knew Honey's childhood hadn't been pleasant. For once, Pauline didn't argue. Instead, she said, "I need to get back to the office. Do you have Horace's manuscript? I used that as an excuse to slip out and meet you."

"Yes, it's right here." Honey handed Pauline the wrapped package. "I'm so glad we can entrust it to you. Horace is such a fine writer, and I'm sure Miss Grimshaw will be impressed. You'll make sure that she reads it, won't you?"

"I'll do my best," Pauline promised. The manuscript was exchanged for a key to Pauline's home. "Come and go as you please," Pauline said. "Shall I tell Mary to expect you for dinner?" Mary had been the Faulkners' housekeeper since Pauline's mother had died.

"I hope we can have dinner with Mike," said Honey. "I won't know until he gets off work. According to his letter, he works in a warehouse by a pier near our old neighborhood and stays in a nearby hotel. There wasn't a phone number in his letter, so I thought we would check the warehouse where he works. The workday down at the pier begins early, so he should be off about four o'clock."

Judy thought Mike expected Honey. Judy had not heard about hanging around a warehouse in the shabby section of the city and hoping for a chance meeting. What if Mike didn't appear?

CHAPTER XIII

Mike and Memories

"Isn't Mike expecting you?" Judy asked after the girls had unpacked and were settled in Pauline's spacious guest room.

"Mike expects me but not necessarily today. He asked me to come whenever I could. Judy, it was so good to get his letter and hear about the neighborhood. He mentioned our old friends and said they had asked about me. Our favorite sandwich shop is still in business. They served the best grilled cheese sandwiches." Honey sounded wistful.

Judy was surprised because she always assumed that Honey had forgotten her old life and wasn't interested in the neighborhood she had left behind.

Honey looked at her watch and said, "We need to hurry if we want to be down at the pier before the workday is over. Let's take a cab," she suggested.

"It seems too early," Judy said.

"The workday starts early at warehouses. Remember, I lived on a street near the warehouses and watched the workmen carry their lunch boxes to and fro." When Honey saw the look on Judy's face, she added. "No, I guess you wouldn't remember. Only Mike would."

Oliver, the Faulkners' butler, hailed a cab, and soon the two friends were crossing the East River into Brooklyn. Honey watched the streets carefully until she declared, "We are almost there. It shouldn't be long now."

The excitement in Honey's voice revealed how much she was anticipating her reunion with Mike Vincenzo. Judy searched the crowd of workers while she waited for Honey to pay the cab driver. She still felt uneasy about the lack of a definite time and place to meet Mike. Honey, however, walked ahead with confidence, and after only a block she called out to a tall, dark-haired man. He turned and eagerly came toward them.

After the young man had given Honey an exuberant hug, he turned to Judy.

"I bet you don't recognize me," he said. "I was just a little kid when you saw me last."

"You have changed," Judy agreed. Instead of

a teenager, a man used to the rigors of hard farm labor stood before her.

"You look the same," Mike said. "Same red hair. Sis showed me pictures from your wedding."

Mike turned back to Honey. "I feel terrible about leaving Pennsylvania without seeing you, but I knew you would worry if I told you before I had another job. Farm jobs are scarce these days, and the two Bradford plants didn't have openings. Coming back to the city seemed the best option."

"I understand now," said Honey. "I can't wait to catch up on all your news. Please have dinner with us tonight. I want to show Sloan's Diner to Judy, and it will seem funny eating there if you aren't with me."

"Sure," Mike grinned. "Betty is still working there. She's missed you."

Judy and Honey followed Mike back to his hotel so he could change clothes and leave his lunch box. Mike then led them to a small, clean diner. It had a long counter with stools and four booths. Mike chose the booth farthest from the door, and Judy noticed that the red vinyl seats contained hairline cracks.

The waitress greeted Honey with, "Will you have the usual?" Although the question sounded routine, the woman's misty eyes and welcoming smile conveyed her delight in seeing Honey.

"Yes, please," Honey smiled with pleasure.

After the waitress left with their orders, Honey whispered, "Betty did remember me, just as you said, Mike."

"Have I ever lied to you?" asked Mike.

"No."

"Well, I don't plan to start now."

Honey's usual turned out to be the grilled cheese sandwich she had mentioned earlier and a small order of fries. Judy could see why Mike and Honey would like this diner. The place was small enough not to be intimidating to children, and the cheap food was filling.

"Did you eat here often?" Judy asked. Even if you included places like diners, the Boltons rarely ate out when she was growing up.

"Whenever Mike or I had money. Mike earned some by running errands. Once a teacher gave me a dollar for staying after school and helping her."

"Sometimes Betty fed me in exchange for sweeping up," Mike recalled. "Until I returned, I had forgotten how good the neighbors were to us."

"Yes, they were," Honey reflected. "Who have you seen?"

Mike hesitated. "The Goldins and the Costas. They're still living on our street."

"Any news?"

"Ma is not doing well."

"What do you mean?" asked Honey.

"Just what I said. I wasn't given any details and I wasn't ready to ask. Being back here has made me think a lot about our childhood. At the time I knew it wasn't normal, but now I know it was crazy. I've wondered about a lot of things."

"I know what you mean," said Honey. "Was Ma forced to steal? Would she be different if given a chance?"

Mike hesitated before replying. "I'm not sure I want to know. I like my new life and don't want to feel obligated to come back and help her."

Judy always knew that Honey had a soft heart. Honey proved it with her next words. "I like my life, too, Mike, but it doesn't help to pretend that our previous lives didn't exist. People helped us—gave us a chance—or we might have come to the point where we didn't care about right or wrong."

"I guess you're right. You always were. I'll see if I can find out what's going on."

"Thanks, and let me know." Honey pulled out a slip of paper and wrote Pauline's address and phone number. "We are staying here while we're in town."

Honey turned the conversation to Horace and their hopes. No more was said about the Vincenzos until they parted ways on the street. Honey turned to Mike and said, "Remember your promise and tell me everything, no matter how bad it is."

After she and Honey were in bed that night, Judy presented the question that had plagued her while they were at the diner. Some things were easier to talk about in the dark.

"You never mention your life before you came to Farringdon. Have you thought about it much?" asked Judy.

"I didn't when I first started living with Peter and our grandparents. Everyone was so good to me, and it was thrilling to start over. The only thoughts of my old life were selfish ones, how I had been cheated out of beautiful things and people who cared about me. As time went by, occasionally something or someone would trigger a memory."

"I thought I had a hard time starting over in Farringdon, but I never realized what it was like for you to move hundreds of miles away and leave everything and everyone behind. I thought your old life didn't matter because you had a happier life," Judy explained.

"I used to think that. I'm glad I moved to Farringdon, but I can't pretend New York didn't exist. I did that for too long. Thinking I had lost touch with Mike made me understand how desperately I needed a connection to my life in Brooklyn," explained Honey.

"I think I understand. My parents, Horace, Peter, your grandparents—we all have the same Roulsville memories, but none of us shares your old memories. Mike is the only one who does."

"Exactly," said Honey. "It sounds obvious,

but it isn't. I missed that truth for a long time. Not only do I love Mike, but I need him."

"Did going to art school in the city bring back memories?" asked Judy.

"Not art school itself because it was in a different part of town. However, I thought about the old neighborhood. I knew Peter would take me for a visit, but I kept making the excuse that he was too busy, when I knew there was another reason. That is why I had to come now."

"I thought you came because of Mike," said Judy.

"I did want to see Mike," Honey said at last. But it's more than that. You always say a person shouldn't run from a ghost. She should walk up to it, face her fear, and expose it for a fraud. I have to face my fear. I need to learn more about my past, and there's only one person who can help me with the missing pieces."

"And that person is a ghost?" asked Judy, bewildered.

"She's worse than a ghost," Honey replied, with a slight shudder. "She's Marie Vincenzo. The woman who raised me."

Judy was dismayed. She liked solving mysteries, and the mystery of Mike Vincenzo was solved when Honey received his letter. The only reason Judy had come to New York was to keep busy while Peter was gone. She was prepared to see Mike, but was she ready to see the thieving Mrs.

Vincenzo and her violent sons? She didn't think so.

"I don't know how you want me to help you," Judy said.

"You'll know what to do when the time comes. You always do. Right now, I just need moral support.

"Horace should be here. He's great at that."

A sweet smile formed on Honey's face. "Horace wants to help me face my past. He wants me to be able to talk freely about it. That's the main reason he regrets not being able to come."

Honey reached across the bed and squeezed Judy's hand. "I know you will be a big help."

Even with Honey's encouraging words, Judy still did not want to visit Mrs. Vincenzo. However, her recent conversations with Horace and Honey had made her more sensitive to Honey's needs. Judy remembered the winter her friends had gone to lectures in order to find a blackmailer. Maybe they hadn't been as interested in solving the mystery as she was, but they had willingly acquiesced to Judy's request. She might not be as interested in the Vincenzo family as Honey was, but she resolved to show the same kindness that had been shown to her.

"I still don't know how I can help you with your 'ghost,' as you call her, but I'll do my best," promised Judy.

It wasn't long before Judy heard Honey's

steady breathing and knew she was asleep. Judy wished she could fall asleep as easily. If it weren't a cold December night, Judy would have stepped out on the roof garden. Looking down on the city lights always made New York seem more thrilling than it was on the actual streets. Tonight she wanted the serenity of looking up at the stars in order to calm her troubled thoughts.

So much had happened since Horace had driven them to the bus station that morning. If only Peter would call and be allowed to talk about the mysterious man. And exactly where was Peter?

CHAPTER XIV

Antique Shopping

"I want to invite Sylvia to dinner while you are here. Are you available tonight?" Pauline asked the next morning.

"I'm not sure," said Judy. "Honey might want to have dinner with Mike again."

"Invite him to join us," offered Pauline.

"I'll ask Honey." Even though Judy had been the last one to fall asleep, she was the first one down to breakfast. "I appreciate your letting us stay with you."

"I enjoy your company, especially with Father gone," said Pauline. "I'm surprised you didn't bring a mystery with you."

Judy had not had an opportunity to tell Pauline about the robbery or the encounter with the man resembling Peter. She wasn't sure she should say anything about the latter. Honey's appearance saved her from answering.

"Speaking of mysteries, did Miss Grimshaw say anything about Horace's manuscript?" asked Honey.

"She said it was better than the other hogwash she had seen this week. Knowing my boss, I would take that as a compliment," said Pauline.

"Pauline wants us to have dinner with Sylvia tonight," said Judy. "I mentioned Mike, and he is welcome to join us."

"How nice. I'll ask him," promised Honey.

"Do you think he might want to talk to your former neighbors this evening?" asked Judy.

"No, he'll go on his lunch hour. My brother doesn't put things off. We can see him after work and invite him," said Honey.

"Good. I'll call Sylvia and ask her to come," said Pauline. "Now if the rest of the day goes as smoothly as these plans, I'll be happy."

"I take it Emily Grimshaw has not been in a good mood lately," said Judy.

"That is an understatement," Pauline replied.

"I'd like to meet her," said Honey.

"I keep forgetting that you weren't here on my other visits," said Judy. "Your trip to New York isn't complete without seeing the witch hunched over her steaming cauldron."

Pauline laughed at Honey's puzzled expression when Judy referred to the unique door knocker on Miss Grimshaw's door. "Judy is not referring to my boss, but I'm not going to tell you what she means. You have to come and see for yourself. I had better leave now or I'll be late to see the witch."

Judy and Honey lingered over breakfast after Pauline's departure. "The other night Peter suggested that I check some of the antique shops here. Local pawnshops fence stolen jewelry and antiques, and Peter says those items often find their way to New York City."

"Oh, Judy, it would be wonderful to find your dishes and dolls!" exclaimed Honey. "That must also mean that Peter thinks the robbery was committed by an ordinary thief."

"I was thinking the opposite," said Judy. "Maybe Peter knows about the link between pawnshops in Pennsylvania and antique stores here because of his current assignment."

"But doesn't the FBI deal with stolen goods crossing state lines all the time?"

"Yes," Judy admitted. "I guess I don't have proof that the robbery was caused by our lunch conversation."

"I hope it wasn't," said Honey. "I don't like to think that my careless talk caused your trouble."

"It wasn't just you. It was my idea in the first place, and I wasn't as careful as I should have been. Are you up for exploring?"

"Yes. Horace and I like the modern styles best, but I might find something interesting for our future home. Where do we start?" asked Honey.

"I have no idea," said Judy. "We'll have to look in the phone book."

Just then, Oliver entered the room. "Would you like more coffee or anything else for breakfast?" he inquired.

"Breakfast was perfect, but perhaps you can help us with something else," Judy said. "We want to explore antique shops. Do you have any suggestions?"

"Miss Pauline and her friends like to shop in Lenox Hill on the Upper East Side. It's easy to reach by bus, or I can call a cab."

"If you don't mind, Honey, I'd like to take the bus so we can stop along the way if we see anything interesting," said Judy.

"A bus sounds fine to me," agreed Honey.

"The Fifth Avenue bus will take you there," offered Oliver. "You only have to walk a few blocks up 23rd Street to catch it. Lenox Hill starts across from Central Park. There are some very nice antique shops for the next few blocks. The bus passes Rockefeller Center in case you care to stop and see our famous Christmas tree."

It didn't take long for the girls to bundle up in their winter coats and head out with Judy's antique list in hand. At Oliver's suggestion, Judy had written a description of the missing items on the back of Pauline's old calling cards. Judy had also added her own name.

"I'll study the list while we are on the bus," said Honey. "I want to help all I can."

From Gramercy Park it was only a short walk to Fifth Avenue, and soon the sisters-in-law were seated together on the bus headed uptown.

"Look, Judy, the stone lions are wearing big Christmas wreaths," Honey pointed out as the bus passed in front of the public library.

Most of the passengers on the bus were businesspeople with their noses in their newspapers, but Judy and Honey were having fun looking at the gaily decorated store windows. In one, toy soldiers formed a marching band while another displayed a little Alpine village with several trains running through it. All of Fifth Avenue seemed to sparkle.

"I had planned to familiarize myself with your list of antiques while we rode, but I don't want to miss the Christmas sights," said Honey.

The girls continued to admire the festive windows as the bus made its way through a sea of cars and yellow taxicabs.

"If you find any of your antiques, how will you prove they belong to you?" asked Honey.

"The Wedgwood will be hard but not the dolls. When my mother heard that the dolls had been stolen, she told me that a cloth tag with the doll's name was sewn onto each doll's chemise.

Mother said she would try to remember the dolls' names."

"That would definitely be helpful," said Honey. "Here comes Rockefeller Center on our left."

"And there's Tiffany's! This must be where the millionaires shop," laughed Judy.

When Judy spotted Central Park on their left, she pulled the string that signaled the driver to stop.

"Oh, this is charming," Honey remarked as they started down the first street. "These antique shops look like they were converted from old houses. Where shall we start?"

"How about here," suggested Judy. "Grandma's sewing machine would fit right in with this window display."

As soon as the girls were inside, they realized they had chosen a store that specialized in furniture. "Look," said Judy with delight. "This desk is identical to the one in the corner of my living room."

"It is," agreed Honey.

"Grandma Smeed let me keep my books there when I visited during the summers. Now it holds my childhood favorites, such as the Oz books."

"I couldn't help overhearing that you own a Georgian oak bureau bookcase," said a nearby salesman. "You have a fine piece of furniture, madam. This is my favorite feature." He pulled down a drop leaf, revealing pigeonholes for filing papers.

Judy stifled a gasp when she looked at the price tag. Her grandmother's desk was a treasure, and not just because it was a family heirloom. The girls thanked the salesman and left for another store. After all, their objective wasn't furniture.

"There are still plenty of shops to look in," Honey encouraged after they left the fourth shop.

"I feel like I am spoiling your plans," said Judy. "Are you sure you want to keep looking?"

"Absolutely. No matter how reassuring you are, I still feel responsible for my carelessness when we spoke with that man I called the Un-Peter," sighed Honey. "And the dishes and dolls are part of your heritage, and Horace's too."

At the next shop, an old-fashioned Santa in a hooded velvet robe stood by the door as if ready to wish them a Merry Christmas.

"He doesn't fit in our budget," Judy noted ruefully after glancing at the price tag.

"Nor mine, but he certainly appeals to me," said Honey as the girls stepped into the shop and began looking at the displays.

"Oh, look," Judy called to Honey. "These antique dolls are similar to the ones that were stolen."

"It looks like their heads and limbs are china," noted Honey as she examined one of the dolls more closely. "This one's body must be cotton."

Judy and Honey examined each doll, but none of them had a name sewn to its chemise.

"This one is adorable," said Honey. "Look at her lace petticoat and matching pantaloons."

"I see you chose the only doll with honey-colored hair," teased Judy. "One of Grandma's dolls was blonde."

I couldn't help overhearing your comment," interjected a nearby saleswoman. "Blonde dolls like that are very rare. Does your doll have a painted-on corset?"

"I don't know," Judy replied. "I inherited the dolls a few years ago and never really examined them. Now they've been stolen," she continued, handing the woman one of the calling cards. "Here's my information."

"Oh, how awful," commiserated the saleswoman. "You won't find any stolen items here, of course. I hope you've contacted the police and your insurance agent."

"My husband is taking care of those details," Judy assured her.

"Look here, Judy," called Honey from the next aisle. "This doll has a china head and a leather body."

"She is just like the doll in one of the photographs we found when we were searching for Grandma's will!" Judy exclaimed. Were they close to recovering some of her stolen items?

CHAPTER XV

Pauline's Dinner Party

"Do you think we have found one?" whispered Honey.

"There's only one way to be sure."

Judy started to lift the doll's petticoat when she was interrupted by the same saleswoman who had continued to hover nearby. "That doll does not have a corset, dear." Her tone was cordial but implied, "Please do not handle our expensive dolls."

Thankfully, the saleswoman's attention was diverted by a customer who was ready to pay for her selections.

"Is she looking?" asked Judy after a few moments.

"No, she's ringing up the sale. Go ahead," urged Honey.

Quickly Judy peeked at the muslin chemise. No name.

"Don't be discouraged," Honey reassured her. "Look, that sign says there's another room upstairs."

The second floor contained items from Judy's mother's generation, not the china bisque dolls displayed below. As they were about to leave the store, Honey called Judy's attention to a shelf of tiny china dolls. "Did you have any dolls like these, Judy?" she asked.

"Yes, there was one with a bonnet like this one. She reminded me of Little Bo Peep. But you couldn't sew a name on her dress. She is solid china."

"I see you have found the standing Charlottes." Their persistent saleswoman had returned. "Did I hear you say that you have a bonnet doll like this one?"

"Yes, I do, or rather, I did."

"You certainly had a nice collection." She handed Judy a business card. "If you are interested in replacing your dolls, please keep us in mind."

The girls continued the search for the remainder of the morning. Some shops had taken only moments to peruse, while a few had required intense scrutiny.

"Something may turn up after all," comforted Honey. "You left your name and Pauline's number at each place. Maybe a shop owner will receive something later this week and call."

"No. It was been three days since the robbery. A criminal wouldn't want to be in possession of stolen goods that long. The UnPeter should have disposed of them by now," said Judy.

"Are you sure it was him?" asked Honey.

"I've decided that it had to be," stated Judy. She hadn't told anyone but Peter about the missing wedding photograph. "Maybe my grandmother's items were sold in Pennsylvania."

"Even if we didn't find what we were looking for, at least we learned more about your dolls."

"Yes, and you bought those pretty glass candlesticks in the crystal shop."

"How could anyone resist such Christmassy, quaint shops?" smiled Honey.

"What do you want to do for the rest of the day?"

"How about buying some hot dogs in Central Park?" suggested Honey. "The sun is out, and we can eat as we walk to the bus."

"And the bus will take us . . . where?" asked Judy.

"To Rockefeller Center. At this time of year, the sunken plaza becomes a skating rink, and the Christmas tree is enormous," Honey explained. "Wait until you see the Golden Statue. There's a quote I want to copy down for Horace, but you can only read if you are on the rink. It's a perfect day to skate, cold but sunny and no wind."

When the Golden Statue finally came into view, Honey explained "It's Prometheus bringing fire to mankind. Wait until you see it close-up."

As soon as they were on the ice, Honey and Judy skated over to the statute.

"Prometheus, teacher in every art, brought the fire that hath proved to mortals a means to mighty ends," read Judy from the granite wall behind the figure.

Honey wrote the inscription in her notebook and added some sketches before circling around the rink.

"Skating is good for me," said Judy. "Flying around the ice makes me feel as carefree as a bird."

"I might feel that way too if I didn't keep stumbling. I would be even worse if Horace hadn't given me skating lessons on the pond at home."

Skating occupied the girls until Honey looked at her watch and announced it was time to go.

"I needed the exercise. It worked off my jitters," said Honey as she and Judy exchanged their skates for their shoes.

"Why the jitters?" asked Judy.

"I guess I'm worried about what Mike learned today. Honey hesitated. "I think I should meet Mike alone and bring him back to Pauline's."

"Are you sure you will be safe?" Judy understood that Honey wanted to talk with Mike privately, but she couldn't help but worry.

"Mike will take care of me. He'll be getting off work when I arrive, and if he doesn't want to come for dinner, he will still see me safely back to Pauline's."

When Judy hesitated, Honey became more insistent. "I'll take a cab to the neighborhood if that will reassure you."

"That would make me feel better," Judy admitted.

After Honey was inside a taxi, Judy walked to her bus stop. Once aboard, she took the first empty seat. Although her body was resting for the first time that day, her brain kept racing along. The morning's search had been disappointing. During the entire ride, she pondered what she should do next."

Oliver greeted Judy at the door. "Were there any phone calls for me?" she inquired.

"No, Mrs. Dobbs."

Peter had not returned her call. Had he even received her message?

Judy went into the sitting room and found Pauline at her desk, cutting envelopes with a small pair of scissors.

"I can stop anytime," said Pauline. "Sylvia gave me a new address book for my birthday, and I saved the envelopes from my Christmas cards so I could paste in the return addresses. Not only does it save time, but I love seeing the handwriting from all my friends or else their pretty printed labels."

"What a great idea! I'll have to remember that tip," said Judy. "The holidays were so hectic that some of my cards are sitting unopened on the kitchen table."

"You can still enjoy them when you get home."

"That's right," agreed Judy, although she knew it wouldn't seem the same.

Judy wasn't sure how to fill the time until dinner. She could call Roulsville and see if the police had any new information.

"Is Mike coming?" asked Pauline.

"I'm not sure. Honey went by herself to see him."

"I hope he comes. It would be fun to find a man for Sylvia. Maybe a friend will return the favor for me one day." Pauline sighed wistfully before continuing. "I'm looking forward to this dinner. It's been a long time since I've had my own friends over. Christmas entertaining usually revolves around Father's associates."

Judy read a few chapters of a manuscript that Pauline had brought home from work while her friend worked on her address book. When Pauline had finished her project, Honey had still not arrived. Judy couldn't telephone Mike because Honey had the phone number in her purse.

"If only I could remember the name of Mike's

hotel," Judy thought. She was about to open Brooklyn's huge phone book to look through the list of hotels when Honey came into the bedroom.

"Mike's staying for dinner," Honey announced. She pulled Mike's box of chocolates from her suitcase and sat it on the bed. "I'll slip on a fresh dress and be down in a minute. Sylvia arrived as we did and is keeping him company."

The evening was fun. Mike fit into the group easily, and the conversation flowed. Sylvia told them about her current interest.

"I knew I couldn't live at home forever, so I decided to take a college course. I loved my introductory psychology class, and when the professor mentioned that art therapy was an innovative way to explore the unconscious, I was intrigued. It turns out that the pioneer in the field teaches at New York University."

"So, what exactly is art therapy?" asked Honey.

"It's a lot of things. I'll be able to tell you more after I've had more classes, but in simple terms, it is using art to help people communicate or deal with trauma or illness or aging. How adults and children either respond to art or create art can tell you much about what they are thinking," Sylvia explained.

"My teachers never understood the things I drew," joked Mike. "I wonder what my childhood art would have said about me."

"Your drawings said many things," Sylvia

told him. "Each person expresses himself differ-
ently."

"I've heard Father talk about it. He believes
art therapy may be very useful in the future, especially after more research has been done," said
Pauline.

"It sounds fascinating," said Judy. The work-
ings of the human mind always intrigued her.

"So, soon you will be an art therapist," said
Honey.

"Not soon," Sylvia sighed. "It will take long
enough for me to get my bachelor's degree, and
art therapy requires a graduate degree. I am not
sure I want to stay in school that long. I'll decide
one semester at a time."

"If you are thinking about having Sylvia use
art therapy to solve mysteries, I guess you will
have to wait," laughed Pauline. "It is a good thing
you don't have any mysteries to solve."

"I actually do have one." Judy told them about
the robbery of her home, although she left out her
chief suspect.

"I can understand Judy taking a holiday jaunt
to the big city while Peter is away, but I am surprised you left Horace," Sylvia said to Honey.
"From your last letter it sounded like things were
getting serious."

"We are serious, which is why I came. Before
I make any marriage plans, I want to visit the old
neighborhood and, if possible, see the woman

who raised me."

"Really?" Sylvia's face showed her surprise. "When will you do that?"

"I'm not sure. Mike went today, but no one answered the door. We think something is up."

"Why?" asked Sylvia.

Mike was the one to answer her question. "According to the neighbors, someone should have been home."

"So you didn't learn anything?" asked Judy.

Mike and Honey exchanged a long look before Honey spoke. "We did learn one thing from a neighbor, but it's rather spooky."

CHAPTER XVI

A Night Visit to the Cemetery

"I really did have a sister named Rose," announced Mike. "She died as an infant, and Ma pretended that Sis was Rose."

The shocking announcement left the group silent. "Rose Vincenzo" wasn't a made-up name for Grace Thompson's daughter. She was a real baby who had died. Mrs. Vincenzo had switched her own dead infant for the living baby of her deceased tenant.

"How did you find this out?" asked Sylvia.

"Some neighbors suspected the switch because I didn't have the coloring or distinctive features of the rest of the family," said Honey. "Today when Mike told Mrs. Costa I belonged to a family in Pennsylvania, she told Mike what she and some others always thought. It makes sense. Why else would a poor woman take on another child? I may have cooked and cleaned when I was older, but I couldn't have been any use to her as a baby."

"Why didn't the neighbors say something before now?" asked Judy.

"Maybe they were afraid. I guess there wasn't any proof," Mike conjectured. "Mrs. Costa asked how I knew, and I told her Sis's thumbprint matched the thumbprint of a baby belonging to a woman who rented rooms from Ma. That was enough, even though . . ." Mike hesitated.

"Even though what?" asked Judy.

"Even though they had been to my graveside service," Honey interjected.

Mike continued the story. "After little Rose died, Ma went around the neighborhood and told everyone she wanted to help a renter who couldn't afford to bury her child. She raised enough money to bury little Grace Thompson, but it was really Rose Vincenzo she was burying. Mrs. Costa said the neighbors helped because Ma was doing something positive for a change, and they hoped their support would change Ma's life. The local church also helped. It wasn't until Honey was older that they became suspicious."

"It may have been a convenient coincidence that Honey's mother eventually died," said Sylvia.

"No," said Judy. "I'm sure that Honey's mother died first."

"Judy's right," said Honey. "The telegram Mrs. Vincenzo sent said 'Morgue has wife's body. Baby dying.'"

"Rose must have died soon after the telegram was sent," said Judy. "I always thought Vine never mentioned the baby to Peter's grandparents, but Mrs. Vincenzo may have been the source of deceit. I guess we will never know."

"Can you believe that somewhere there is a grave with my name on it?" asked Honey.

Even practical, unemotional Pauline had to agree that a grave with Honey's name was spooky.

"Could it be found?" wondered Honey.

"Mrs. Costa told me where it is," Mike stated. "It's in a church cemetery near the old neighborhood."

"I'm going to go and see it," declared Honey.

"When?" asked Pauline.

"Anytime. I'm ready to go now."

"At night?" asked Sylvia incredulously. "I've never been in a cemetery before and certainly not at night."

Judy was also reluctant, but her reticence wasn't because it was dark or involved a cemetery. Tonight she hoped that Peter would call. They could see the gravestone anytime. Mike knew where to find it, and it would be there tomorrow.

"I don't mind being in a cemetery at night, but would it be safe to travel there after dark?" asked Pauline.

"A taxi would be safe," insisted Honey.

No more objections were raised. As soon as dessert was finished, the group was out on the street hailing a taxi. Even new snowflakes had not deterred them.

"Here's a ride now," said Honey as a cab finally slowed at Mike's signal.

"Isn't that how it always is," Pauline said as she took the last spot in the back seat and looked out the back window. "We have to wait longer than usual for a taxi, and another comes by right after this one."

"He's dropping off a passenger," observed Mike. He closed Pauline's door and climbed in front with the driver.

"What if the cemetery is locked?" Sylvia asked eventually.

"I don't think it will be," said Mike. "It's small, so it might not even have a fence."

"You were right, Mike. It's unlocked," called Honey when she pushed open the gate. Slushy snow filled the spaces between the headstones. The older graves looked grim and neglected.

"I'm thankful the snow isn't sticking to the stones," said Sylvia. "I wouldn't want to clean each one to read the names."

"I'm thankful this place is small," said Pauline after they had surveyed all the rows in the first section. "Otherwise we could be here all night, and I do have to report to work tomorrow."

There weren't any street lamps bordering the cemetery, and it was a moonless night. Few cars and their accompanying headlights were on the side street. "If we are counting blessings, I'm thankful I brought a flashlight," said Mike.

Honey and Mike headed for the first row in the next section and began reading the names. Finally, they paused before a small marker. "I've found my gravestone," Honey whispered. "Grace Thompson. It's surreal seeing it here. It is also strange seeing the name Thompson instead of Dobbs. It's so...plain. There's my name, date of birth, and date of death. Nothing else. I don't know why, but I expected more."

Judy glanced at the white marble slab with Honey's name on it. There was nothing frightening about it, but she shivered nonetheless.

"It's not your grave," Judy reminded her. "It's Rose Vincenzo's grave."

"Yes, and her mother did what she had to do for her daughter to have a decent burial. She never seemed like a mother to me, but she must have had some motherly feelings. She couldn't have been all bad."

"Maybe that's the whole point of your journey," said Judy slowly. "People and situations are complex. People do the wrong things for the right reasons. Your grandparents loved their daughter and wanted to protect her, so they were too strict. Maybe if they'd trusted Grace's judgment

"I've found my gravestone," Honey whispered.

and gotten to know James, Grace wouldn't have rebelled and eloped with him."

"And if my parents really loved each other, they could have waited," added Honey. "Instead, they chose to run away. We blame others for our decisions, but ultimately we make our own choices."

"Do you still want to see Mrs. Vincenzo?" Judy asked. "Or would you rather move on?"

"I can't change the past by pretending it never happened," Honey replied. "For some reason I really have to see Ma. Now I realize that she needed me, and I have some sympathy for her. After all, she lost a baby daughter. I want to understand what she was feeling."

"Understanding feelings—isn't that what art therapy is all about?" Pauline asked. "It won't solve Judy's mystery, but it might solve yours, Honey."

"You're right," agreed Honey. She turned to Sylvia. "Would you be willing to help?"

"I know a professor who has a grant to learn how art helps people become more comfortable discussing their feelings and events in their lives. Maybe Mrs. Vincenzo could become part of his project. If not, he might know of another person or an agency that can help. I can find out more tomorrow," offered Sylvia. "Professors usually work on their research projects during holiday breaks."

After everyone had looked at the gravestone, there didn't seem to be any purpose in sticking around. The group walked Sylvia to the nearest subway stop, and then Mike hailed a taxi for the girls before he walked to his hotel. A quiet group returned to the Faulkner house, a group that was more somber than the one that had left a few hours earlier.

CHAPTER XVII

Honey Sees the Witch

JUDY'S eyes flew open. She had fallen asleep quickly, but something had awakened her. Was it just the wind or something else? Judy pulled on her long rose robe and peered out the nearest window. All she saw was snow falling more heavily than before. Taking care not to wake Honey, she moved to another window and looked out in both directions. A few cars were slowly navigating the snowy streets. Judy's ears perked up. Was it her imagination, or did she hear a noise coming from the roof garden?

Judy stepped into her boots and threw her coat over her shoulders. Silently she slipped out the door and into the living area that separated Pauline's suite from the guest room. She unlocked the door and stepped onto the roof garden, startling a group of pigeons who flew off in a whoosh of flapping wings. The gravel crunched beneath her feet. What had awoken her? Was it the sound of the gravel, the pigeons, or something more ominous?

The claw prints of the pigeons made a pretty pattern in the snow, but Judy couldn't discern any human footprints other than her own. She made her way between the wicker chairs to the edge of the garden. From her third-story perch, she had a magnificent view of the neighborhood and, farther off, the skyscrapers that defined the city. Looking down, she saw a solitary, tall figure walking rapidly toward Fifth Avenue. Could it be the UnPeter? If so, why would he be keeping an eye on the Faulkners' home?

Judy looked up at the midnight sky, but the stars were silent and offered no answers. A blast of wintry wind convinced her to retreat indoors.

As Judy slipped back into the bedroom, the luminous face of the bedside clock showed that only an hour had passed since she had gone to bed. It seemed like the middle of the night. Judy removed her dampened coat and boots and hung her robe up to dry, since the trailing ends had become wet with snow. Still wondering what had disturbed her sleep, Judy climbed back into bed.

"Did you sleep well?" asked Judy at breakfast. She really wondered if Honey or Pauline had heard anything during the night.

"No. I had some really strange dreams," said Honey. "I called Horace this morning and told him about everything that happened yesterday. He said my restless night was from trying to process my experiences. He thinks dreams help us deal with problems we can't solve while we are awake."

"Then I wish I would dream about what to do with an annoying author," complained Pauline. "He and Miss Grimshaw rub each other the wrong way, so I have to be the one to work with him."

"Maybe he should find another agent," suggested Honey.

"No, he brings in too much money to lose as a client, and he knows my boss gives him the best advice," Pauline said. "Stop by today and maybe you'll meet them both."

"I'd like that," said Honey.

"I can't wait for you to finish breakfast, or I'll be late for my appointment with the witch and her cauldron. Come by later if you are brave enough," teased Pauline as she grabbed her briefcase.

"You're not scaring me," retorted Honey.

"It's not too far to walk, and I want to check out the neighborhood," Judy said when she and Honey were ready to leave. "Last night I heard a noise, and when I investigated, I saw a tall figure walking away from the house.

"Lots of people walk at night in Manhattan," Honey reminded her.

"True, but you know how curious I am. I'm not sure what I'm looking for, but if something is amiss, perhaps we will see it." However, the walk to Pauline's office gave Judy and Honey exercise but nothing else.

"Doesn't this look and sound like the residence of a witch?" asked Judy while they rode the creaky elevator to a dark hallway on the fourth floor of Pauline's building.

Honey laughed when she saw the one-of-a-kind witch-and-cauldron door knocker on Emily Grimshaw's door. "I have to sketch this. It's incredible!"

"I'll go inside while you work," said Judy. "Take your time."

"I will. I want to capture this challenging piece from every angle. I hope I can do it justice."

Judy entered the familiar office. Little had changed since she first entered it six years earlier. Miss Emily Grimshaw, seated behind her massive desk, blended in seamlessly with the Victorian furniture.

"It's about time you showed your face," sputtered Miss Grimshaw. "There's nothing to fear. I like your brother's yarn. Tell him I'll send him some comments next week."

"What exciting news!" exclaimed Judy. "He's

worked so hard on it, and I am so proud of him. You should tell my sister-in-law, Honey, when she comes in because she's the one who persuaded him to submit it."

Miss Grimshaw peered over her glasses and gazed at Judy. "So another woman has usurped your place as Horace's representative. Well, tell me, what do you think about that?"

"It's fine with me," laughed Judy.

"You should know, Miss Grimshaw," Pauline said boldly. "Surely you were usurped sometime in your youth?"

"That's neither here nor there," blustered the older woman. "So where is this Honey person?"

"She's outside sketching your door knocker," explained Judy. "She's an artist." If Miss Grimshaw's decision to represent Horace's book had been hanging in the balance, Judy's words would have clinched the deal.

"An artist? Well, it would take someone like that to appreciate my door knocker. My mother found it when she cleaned out the attic for her maiden aunt. Both were going to throw it out, but I took a fancy to it."

"What did your mother think when you hung it on your office door?" asked Pauline.

"I didn't tell her, and she's never been to my office to find out. She believes a woman belongs at home. She'd be in a fine fix now if I weren't a businesswoman."

Judy sensed a good story. Pauline must have felt the same way because she leaned forward and asked, "What do you mean?"

"It's my profits that are paying her medical bills, and those bills keep adding up. She recently inherited the house that belonged to her aunt, the one who gave me the door knocker. If my mother can earn some income from the property, she will be set for a number of years."

"That sounds like a good solution," commented Pauline.

"Thankfully, a good friend just met an investment counselor who might be useful."

If Judy didn't know that the UnPeter was involved in investment fraud, she would have stopped paying attention to the conversation. Now she was attuned to the subject.

"Tell me about this man," Judy urged.

"What makes you think this person is a man? Aren't women smart enough to understand the stock market, interest rates, and such?" demanded the shrewd businesswoman.

"Yes," said Judy, feeling disappointed as well as chastised. She herself had resented others assuming that women couldn't be detectives.

"I would like to meet this woman," said Pauline.

"I didn't say the advisor was a woman. I said that Judy shouldn't assume that the advisor was a man," corrected Miss Grimshaw. "As a matter of fact he is a man, a very charming man from what Amelia tells me."

Judy's ears perked up again at the word charming. "What do you know about this man?" Judy repeated.

"What's there to know?" asked Miss Grimshaw sharply.

"Is he honest?" asked Judy. "He could be involved in a scam."

"Judy, why would you immediately suspect someone whom you have never met?" Pauline asked. "Investment advisors are well trained and have helped Father manage the income from his practice."

Honey's entrance ended the animated conversation. Her enthusiasm over the witch and cauldron sealed Honey's place in Miss Grimshaw's heart. For Honey's benefit, the older woman repeated her story of rescuing the antique.

"Tell Honey the good news," Pauline prompted.

"There's a market for the kind of the stories that Horace spins. I know where I can place it," Miss Grimshaw informed them.

"Thank you so much! I'm thrilled and can't wait to tell him," enthused Honey.

"Feel free to use the phone on my desk. After all, it is a business call and will save me the trouble."

When they were back on the street, Honey

said, "I enjoyed meeting Miss Grimshaw. Thank you for calling attention to the door knocker. You really had me wondering about your witch and cauldron. I wonder how old the door knocker is. It belongs in a museum."

"A door knocker in a museum?" wondered Judy.

"If we have a chance to go to the Metropolitan Museum of Art, I could show you rooms of household furnishings."

"Let's go there now. You spent yesterday helping me browse antique shops, so today it's your turn to choose."

"I would like see the Hopper *Lighthouse*," admitted Honey.

"Now you are the one talking in riddles," said Judy.

"It's not a real lighthouse, just an oil painting by the same artist who painted the people in the diner. It was on one of the cards in the game Horace gave me."

"I remember the painting of the diner, and I'd like to see it up close. Can we?" asked Judy.

"Not unless you want a side trip to the Art Institute of Chicago. Horace said he would take me one day." Honey smiled at the thought. Whether it was more thoughts of Horace or being surrounded by art, Honey seemed perfectly happy that morning as the girls browsed through the many galleries.

Judy wanted to match Honey's mood, but she was anxious to hear from her husband and worried about the whereabouts of the man who resembled him. Occasionally a painting would catch Judy's eye, and she would wonder about the people or objects portrayed, but she was more interested in the real people crowding the galleries during the holiday week. Once she even thought she heard Peter's distinctive cough, but when she scrutinized the crowd, he wasn't there. But, was the UnPeter there? If discussing an art game had caused the break-in, then obviously he knew something about works of art. Of course, he wouldn't case an art museum. A theft should be impossible with the security guards and alarm systems.

"This morning has been wonderful, but I don't think I can absorb any more," Honey finally said.

Judy thought Honey had chosen the perfect word to describe her experience that morning. In contrast to Judy's casual observations, Honey seemed to "absorb" each painting she studied.

"We have all afternoon before we are due back at Pauline's. Would you like to go back to Lenox Hill?" offered Honey.

"No," Judy replied. "I feel we did everything we could there yesterday. "Do you have someplace you would like to go?"

"Yes, but first, I need to get change for a phone call."

After seeing the amount of change Honey

HONEY SEES THE WITCH 149

received in exchange for her bills, Judy knew it
was going to be an expensive long-distance call.
Seeing Honey's expression through the phone
booth window confirmed what Judy had already
guessed: Honey was calling Horace.

"Let's go to my old street. I'm ready to face
it," declared Honey when she had finished her
call. "Since seeing the gravestone, I've been anxious to visit my neighborhood and wondering
what Horace would say about it. He thinks it will
be safe in the daytime if I am with you and we
don't try to enter the house."

Judy could tell that Honey was at peace with
her decision. However, Judy wasn't sure if she
was ready for the Vincenzos.

CHAPTER XVIII

A Day in Brooklyn

THE first thought that struck Judy when she saw Honey's former neighborhood was that Christmas looked different here. The holiday sparkle that permeated Pauline's neighborhood and the tourist areas of New York City had evaded this impoverished section of Brooklyn. Two houses were boarded up and the rest were badly in need of paint and repairs.

"There it is." Honey pointed to a rooming house in the middle of the block.

"Has it changed?" asked Judy.

"I don't know. Maybe it looks different because I've changed. This is no longer normal."

Judy couldn't imagine such a setting ever being normal. With startling clarity, Judy saw the fabric of Honey's early life unraveling before her.

"I can't take it all in at once," said Honey. "Let's walk down to the end of the street, and then we can pass by on the other side."

What a contrast compared to this morning, thought Judy. Honey was not ready to "absorb" this experience. The juxtaposition of the two expeditions made Judy wonder if Honey's childhood had made her the artist she was, more sensitive to beauty, more sensitive to things Judy took for granted.

"Let's not turn around," said Honey when they reached the corner. "I can get a better view of the alley and our backyard if we walk around the block."

Honey stopped when they came to a break between the dwellings lining the street. Judy didn't see a backyard, just some dirt patches where grass was unlikely to grow in the spring.

"Do you mind waiting a minute?" asked Honey. "I told Horace about sketching the door knocker, and he wondered if sketching the old neighborhood would help me. I think he's right."

Honey pulled out her sketch pad and made rapid marks across the page. Eventually she tucked her work back into her purse and said, "I wonder what an art therapist would say about this drawing."

The girls circled back to the house that had brought them to the neighborhood. After a long look, Honey said, "Something is wrong, but I don't know what it is. I'm going to draw the front of the house. Maybe that will help me figure it out."

Judy looked up and down the street while she waited. Faces were looking out the windows, so she and Honey had not gone unnoticed.

"Let's knock on the door across the street," said Honey. "Mrs. Goldin, who always looked out for us, lives there."

"Hi, Rose," the former neighbor greeted Honey.

"Hello, Mrs. Goldin," said Honey. "Mike told me he saw you."

"It was good to see Mike after all these years, and now the chance to see you." They were immediately invited inside to a tidy front room.

"I thought about you while I was away. Thank you for all the kindness you showed me over the years." Honey was poised. If this was an emotional encounter, she wasn't showing it.

"I thought about you, too, and I can't say I wasn't worried when you disappeared."

Honey gave an abbreviated account of the past few years and included the fact that Judy was her sister-in-law. Honey ended by asking her own question. "How's Ma?"

"I can't really tell you. She still lives across the street, but we never see her anymore. She had a bad fall several winters ago and apparently hasn't recovered. She wasn't in the best of health, but she should be better by now."

"Do you ever see the boys?" asked Honey.

"They're hardly boys anymore, dear, and they're just as…" Mrs. Goldin seemed to search for the right word. She glanced at Judy as if she wasn't sure what to reveal. "…As unfriendly as ever. They come and go."

"I want to check on Ma, but when Mike went by yesterday, no one answered the door," said Honey.

"Tony answered the door earlier today and let a man inside," offered the neighbor.

"What did the man look like?" asked Judy.

"Well, he was tall and had short blond hair. He stood on the porch a while before he finally pulled something from his pocket, and after that Tony let him in."

That made sense to Judy. Peter must have been admitted after he showed his credentials. "Did he stay long?" she asked.

"A while. Okay, I admit I watched, but only because I am concerned about some of the goings-on across the street."

Like Honey, Judy kept her poise, although the last bit of information encouraged her. Peter must have come to New York instead of calling her. Maybe she had not imagined hearing him at the art gallery.

"That might have been my husband. He's . . ."

Judy hesitated as she carefully chose her next words. "He's a government official."

"Then I won't worry if I see him again." Mrs. Goldin's eyes were a little misty as she patted Honey's hand. "It is so good to see you, Rose, so good." The two former neighbors hugged before Judy and Honey returned to the street.

"I hope Peter will contact me. If he has a free hour, maybe we could do something together," said Judy.

"Do you really think Peter is here in New York?" asked Honey.

"Yes. I thought I heard him at the art museum, and the description Mrs. Goldin gave just now sounds like him," said Judy.

Honey agreed. She turned and took one last look at the neighborhood. "I've had enough for today," she sighed. "Let's find a coffee shop."

"Isn't the diner where we ate with Mike nearby?" asked Judy.

"It is, but I'd rather go to a more cheerful section of Brooklyn, away from the old neighborhood. We can take the bus to Prospect Park. When I was a little girl, we went there on a school trip to the zoo. I remember gardens full of brilliant flowers."

"We won't find any flowers there in December," Judy reminded her.

"Oh, yes, we will," laughed Honey. "Here comes the bus."

Judy took a seat by the window, and after a few blocks she felt as though they were driving back into Christmas. The tree-lined avenue of brownstone homes was a sharp contrast to the street where Honey had lived as a child. The holiday decorations were simple but elegant.

As soon as they stepped off the bus, Honey chose a café. The waitress seated them by a window that looked across to the greenery of Prospect Park.

"Horace asked me to let him know as soon as I was safely out of the old neighborhood," Honey explained as she excused herself to make the phone call.

When she returned and the waitress had brought bowls of hot soup, Judy decided to broach a sensitive subject. "Did it feel funny to be called Rose?"

"No, the name Rose belongs in the old neighborhood. It would have felt funny for Mrs. Goldin to call me Honey or Grace. When I left Brooklyn, I didn't just move to a new town. I assumed a new identity."

After lunch the two friends walked into the park and along pathways lined with snow-dusted evergreens and holly trees. A pair of cardinals, looking as though they were posing for a Christmas card, perched in the branches.

As they approached one of the conservatories, a wedding party stepped out, the bridesmaids wearing green velvet dresses and sprigs of holly in their hair. The bride was radiant as she tossed her bouquet of red roses in the air.

"I feel like dashing in and catching that bouquet!" laughed Honey. "I wonder what Horace would think of a winter wedding?"

"He will happily marry you on any day you choose," was Judy's response.

Honey led the way into a glass-enclosed conservatory where the heat caused the girls to remove their coats. "Here are the flowers I promised you."

Both girls were drawn to an exhibit of flowering cacti, and soon Honey was busy sketching the prickly plants.

"The gardens really lifted my spirits," said Honey as they left the park an hour later.

Judy agreed, especially since Honey was starting to imagine her own wedding.

Walking toward the bus stop, Honey grabbed Judy's arm. "Look, an antique shop. I'm sure it won't be as exclusive as the ones in Lenox Hill, but it's worth a try."

The bell over the door tinkled as the girls entered the dimly lit store. The lack of light didn't matter. The striking woman with long black hair and wearing a bright pink coat would stand out anywhere. It was the woman who had caused the commotion during the department store robbery!

"Can I help you ladies?" questioned the

proprietor.

"We were looking for a hostess gift," was Judy's quick response.

Honey took the conversation from there, asking for Wedgwood, which allowed Judy the chance to concentrate on their suspect, who was looking at an opal bracelet. Judy anxiously looked for a public phone, but none was in view. While Honey was making a purchase, the woman slipped out of the store. Judy immediately dashed out the door, but she wasn't fast enough. A taxi waiting at the curb pulled away with their suspect inside.

"What happened?" cried Honey as she joined Judy on the sidewalk.

"She's disappeared." Judy couldn't hide the disappointment in her voice. "I've got to call Peter. I'd bet something precious that she stole that jewelry! I'll ask the proprietor if we can use his private phone, and you can tell him what we suspect while I make the call."

Following the all-too-familiar pattern, Judy was unable to reach Peter and had to leave a message at the Field Office. While she was on the phone, the shop owner looked through the jewelry collection and confirmed that an opal necklace and matching bracelet were missing.

The girls spent the next half-hour answering questions from Brooklyn police officers before they were able to board a bus for Manhattan.

When Judy and Honey finally arrived at the

Faulkners', they were surprised to find that Mike and Sylvia were there. Pauline had arranged another dinner party. Judy wondered if her hostess was playing matchmaker. Honey pulled Mike aside while Judy tried to reach Peter again.

At dinner, Judy viewed Mike as Sylvia's prospective suitor. The couple looked cute together, Mike's rugged features and strong build in contrast to Sylvia's slim figure and delicate face. Dark hair was their only physical similarity. More important than looks, were the two well suited for a lifetime together? Mike was hardworking, polite, interested in others, and protective of Honey. His neighbors in Bradford trusted him. Judy could see him making a good husband.

Judy wondered if Sylvia had the same thought when she asked, "Do you want to spend the rest of your life New York City, Mike?"

"I prefer the country and working outdoors, but I'm smart enough to be thankful for a good-paying job no matter where it is."

"I wish you would find something near Farringdon," said Honey.

"That's not likely, Sis, unless you know of a farmer needing help."

"I might know of a job for you," Judy interjected. "A friend said he couldn't keep up with his landscaping business and wanted to hire someone dependable."

"Do you think he meant it?" asked Mike.

"It sounded like he did," replied Judy. "I'll give you Red's phone number and you can contact him."

"I think you would like Red," Honey told Mike. "You two have a lot in common. He used to live in New York City and had some difficult experiences before he came to help Judy's grandparents. He inherited some land from them and used it to begin his business."

"Thank you for the tip, Judy. I'll follow up. Honey told me about you going with her to the old neighborhood today. Hopefully one of us can see Ma soon."

"Speaking of Mrs. Vincenzo, I have good news," Sylvia announced. "I contacted the professor I know and asked him about his current research project. It turns out that he is using the holiday break to gather data. He gave me a questionnaire for Mrs. Vincenzo to fill out. Does anyone want to go with me on a fact-finding mission tomorrow?"

"On New Year's Eve?" scoffed Pauline.

"It's a good time to catch people at home," Sylvia responded. "Some offices close early or people take off work."

"I'm willing to try," said Judy. She wanted to tell the group about Peter's visit to the Vincenzo home but knew she couldn't because his work was confidential. It didn't matter if Peter didn't call right away. He was here in the city with her.

Judy's optimism stayed with her until after everyone left, and Oliver called her to the phone.

"Hi, Angel. It's good to hear your voice," said Peter. "I'm sorry I couldn't call you earlier."

"It's all right," said Judy. "Just knowing that you are nearby is enough."

"I'm not exactly nearby," said Peter.

"I'm in New York City with Honey. Remember?"

"Right, and I haven't left Pennsylvania. In fact I'm in western Pennsylvania, farther from you than ever."

CHAPTER XIX

Phone Calls

"Why did you think I was in New York?" asked Peter.

"First, I thought I heard your voice, and then later...."

"One thing at a time," Peter interrupted. "Where were you when you thought you heard my voice?" asked Peter.

"At the Metropolitan Museum of Art, and then this afternoon Mrs. Goldin—she lives across the street from the Vincenzos—described you when she was telling us about a visitor to their house. I assumed you were there on official business." Judy paused, then added, "Peter, that neighborhood is awful."

"Why were you at the Vincenzo house, and

why should I be there on official business?" asked Peter.

"Which question do you want me to answer first?"

"Take your pick."

Judy had forgotten that Peter had not heard the story of Mike Vincenzo. On Christmas Eve, the shoplifting incident had overshadowed Honey's concerns about Mike. Judy's lunch encounter in Bradford and the robbery at their own home had taken priority during their next conversations.

"Honey was worried about Mike Vincenzo because her Christmas card to him was returned stamped 'address unknown.' That was the reason we drove to Bradford on Saturday. A neighbor said he had moved to New York City."

"And Honey thought he had returned to the Vincenzos?" asked Peter.

"No. She received a letter saying he had a job in Brooklyn."

"I'm afraid I'm not following you," said Peter.

"Worrying about Mike made Honey think about her past, so she wanted to visit the old neighborhood. Honey could explain it better. I can't say I understand everything, Peter, but there is one thing I do understand. Honey has been through more than we realized, both before and after moving to Farringdon. Today we went to her old neighborhood and talked to Mrs. Goldin.

She said a tall man with short blond hair had been admitted to the Vincenzo home, and I concluded it was you."

Peter asked for more details, and then said, "I am not the only tall, blond man in the world. Except for the physical description, is there any particular reason why you connected the Vincenzos to FBI business?"

"She said that the man was admitted after he presented something that seemed like credentials. We both know the Vincenzos' criminal history."

"Anything else?" persisted Peter.

"No, except for past experience. You know how many times my mysteries became intertwined with your assignments." Judy was beginning to feel rather foolish. She never should have told Mrs. Goldin that the man knocking on the Vincenzo door was her husband and a government official.

"Are the Vincenzos your current mystery?" questioned Peter.

"No," admitted Judy. "Honey found Mike right away. Mrs. Vincenzo isn't doing well, and the neighbors haven't seen her in a while, which seems unusual. I don't consider that a mystery. I guess my only mystery is the robbery of our home. I visited some antique shops yesterday to look for Grandma's dolls and Wedgwood."

"Your dolls and your Wedgwood," Peter gently reminded her.

"My dolls and my Wedgwood," Judy repeated. "Did you get my message about seeing the woman from Brandt's?"

"Yes."

Judy waited. "Surely you can tell me something," she persisted when Peter didn't volunteer any information.

"Be careful, and stay out of trouble," teased Peter.

"You know what I mean," Judy retorted.

"Thanks to you, I brought up the point that our man may be a relative. Once the agency knew I was comfortable with that possibility, I was assigned to question interested parties. I've learned some things about my father's parents and met a great-uncle."

"Does that mean that the man you are watching is related to you?"

"Yes, but I can't tell you more than that. Even if I could, I don't want to discuss this over the phone."

"Are you still going to pose as our criminal?" asked Judy.

"I can't tell you that, either, but the missing photo has changed some plans. Your information is valuable, especially seeing the accomplice today. New York wasn't on our radar. That reminds me that starting tomorrow, I have a new number where you can reach me."

Judy wrote down the information on a nearby

tablet and pulled off the top sheet. It was an easy phone number to remember. Did the FBI choose easy numbers on purpose?

Peter ended the conversation with, "Hopefully this will be over soon, and we can be together."

After Judy hung up, she realized she hadn't told Peter about the visit to the cemetery or her planned trip to the Vincenzos with Sylvia. More importantly, she didn't have the answer to her most pressing questions. Was the UnPeter in New York? Was he the man she had seen outside the Faulkner home? It seemed likely because his accomplice was here. If so, had he followed her to New York City or was he here by coincidence? And was he the man at the Vincenzo house today?

The phone rang again and instinctively Judy answered it, even though it was Oliver's job.

"You're just the person I want. I have proof," was the greeting Judy received.

"What do you mean?" asked Judy. Her thoughts were still with Peter and the new topic confused her.

"My friend's investment advisor isn't dishonest," Miss Grimshaw crowed. "I called Amelia today and asked her more questions. Listen to this. He has such a good heart that he even gave her one of his grandmother's antiques."

"He must have a hard heart to give his grandmother's possessions to a stranger," Judy countered. "I would never give away my grandmother's things."

"That's because you are a woman. He's a man. What use does he have for a doll if it can bring a woman pleasure?"

"Doll? What kind of doll?" questioned Judy.

"An old doll. I thought this information would stop the questions, not start more."

"Will you please call your friend and ask her to describe the doll?" asked Judy.

"I'll do no such thing," Miss Grimshaw snapped. "What does it matter to you?"

"It matters a lot. Someone broke into my house and stole my grandmother's doll collection. I mean, the doll collection that my grandmother gave me."

"The salesman gave my friend his grandmother's doll, not your grandmother's doll," sputtered Miss Grimshaw.

"How do you know?" challenged Judy.

The long pause that followed let Judy know she had caught the older woman off guard. "You couldn't prove it if it were the same doll."

"I might prove it," said Judy. "My dolls have their names sewn on their chemises."

"Sounds like a wild-goose chase to me," muttered Miss Grimshaw.

"Please, this means a lot to me," pleaded Judy.

"I'll think about it. It's too late to call Amelia now. I only called you this late because I kept getting a busy signal earlier."

Judy knew she couldn't force Miss Grimshaw to do anything, but she could be prepared in case she did find the doll. Patients called Dr. Bolton during the night, and therefore the Boltons wouldn't be alarmed by a late phone call.

"Mother, have you remembered the names of Grandma's dolls?"

"One was Maybelle. I should have recalled that one right away because it was my favorite name. Have you found the dolls?"

"Probably not, but if I do, I want to be able to prove they are mine."

"I'll try to remember," said Mrs. Bolton. "If I heard the names, I would recognize them. Tell me how Honey is doing. I sense that Horace is worried about her."

Judy filled her mother in on Honey's visit to the old neighborhood as well as the happier times at the art museum and Prospect Park.

"At least I have a clue to consider," Judy thought after their conversation ended. Someone was ingratiating himself with people who had money to invest. There had to be more. This man had to have a bigger plan or else Emily Grimshaw was right. He was simply a nice man caring for the needs of others. Judy went upstairs and sat at the desk in Pauline's sitting room.

The biggest question was whether or not it was the UnPeter who visited the Vincenzos. She knew that a good FBI wife should be content to allow Peter to solve that mystery, but Judy never could ignore a puzzling situation, and she wasn't entirely to blame. The incident in the Brooklyn store and Emily Grimshaw's information proved that the mystery couldn't keep away from her either.

"What is today's strategy?" Pauline asked at breakfast the next morning.

"I want to polish the sketches I made yesterday, and I need to rest," said Honey. "Work was hectic during the Christmas season, and running around New York City has finally caught up with me. I also want to be here in case Horace calls. He hopes he can come for New Year's Day."

"Sylvia is supposed to call later this morning so we can make plans to see Mrs. Vincenzo," said Judy. "I would like to have another chat with Miss Grimshaw as well."

"Come to work with me, Judy," Pauline urged. "Once I meet with my annoying author, I am free for the rest of the day. I thought I would buy a new dress for Irene's New Year's open house tomorrow. I never know who I might meet at a party, and Dale has fascinating friends."

"When I saw Irene's invitation in her Christmas card, I never thought I would be able to attend her open house," Honey said.

Even though Sylvia had mentioned New Year's last night, Judy had forgotten about it, and she certainly didn't know Irene was having a party.

She wondered why she hadn't been invited, and then remembered the unopened Christmas cards back in Dry Brook Hollow.

"I'll call Irene and let her know to count on at least four of us," said Pauline. "Father called and is flying home later today."

"Any plans for tonight?" asked Judy.

"What I want to do is attend a New Year's Eve dance with the man of my dreams," said Pauline. "The hotel where Dale took us dancing the first summer you visited would suit me. However, unless the unknown Prince Charming appears within the next couple of hours, I'll have to be content with watching TV as the New Year's Ball drops on Times Square. It will be fun with Father and all of you."

"If Sylvia or Peter calls, please ask them to reach me at Miss Grimshaw's office," Judy told Oliver before leaving with Pauline.

Judy and Pauline met Miss Grimshaw stepping out of the elevator. "Your appointment is canceled. The author forgot about previous plans—just like him," she told Pauline brusquely. To Judy she said, "I left a note on Pauline's desk for you."

Judy hoped it was good news, and it was. Scribbled on a piece of paper was a phone number and the words "Call Amelia yourself."

CHAPTER XX

A Visit with Amelia

JUDY put down the phone receiver on Pauline's desk. "Amelia isn't available until later in the morning, so I left your home phone number. I wish Miss Grimshaw had given me Amelia's last name. It seems strange to use the first name of an older woman I don't know."

"If Amelia minded, Miss Grimshaw would have told you to call Miss So and So," said Pauline.

"She might be a Mrs. So and So."

"Miss Grimshaw's friends are probably eccentric old maids like herself," said Pauline. "While the office is quiet, I want to organize the papers on my desk. After that, we might as well go home and see if Honey has heard from Horace. If so, she might be willing to leave the house to go shopping with me."

"Speaking of Horace, his book must be good," said Judy.

"You haven't read it?"

"Not a word," Judy replied.

Pauline crossed over to her boss's massive desk and lifted a thick sheaf of papers from a stack. "Here, entertain yourself while I work."

The next hour passed quickly.

"You just missed a call from Miss Sylvia," Oliver told Judy when the girls entered the house. "Your mother also called."

He handed her a piece of paper that said, "Two of the names are Bessie and Daisy. I will call again if I remember any more."

Judy thanked him and said, "I'll call Sylvia back as soon as I talk to Honey."

"I'm right here," said Honey. "Horace called me from the Farringdon bus station and will be here tonight."

"Do you two want to be alone?" asked Pauline coyly. "Judy and I can find something to do."

"We can all be together," laughed Honey. "Do you mind if Mike joins us? Horace and Mike haven't seen each other since I started driving myself to Bradford. I want them to get to know each other better."

"Of course Mike can come, and I know Irene would welcome him tomorrow," said Pauline.

"Her open houses always draw a crowd, so one more won't matter."

Judy called Sylvia next. Because they needed to arrive at the Vincenzos together, Judy suggested that they meet at Sloan's Diner at one o'clock.

"I'll put Honey on the phone, and she can tell you how to find the diner." Judy copied down Honey's directions as well. She didn't want to be lost in the Vincenzo neighborhood.

Judy was tucking the directions into her purse when Oliver called her to the phone. This time it was Amelia.

"I'm a friend of Emily Grimshaw," Judy explained. "I'm interested in antique dolls because my grandmother left me a collection that has been in the family for years. Yesterday Miss Grimshaw mentioned that you recently acquired an antique doll, and I wondered if you would tell me about it."

"I would love to. The only antique Emily is interested in is her wicked door knocker. If you love dolls, you should come and see my entire collection."

"I'd love to, but I'm only in town for a short time. I'm staying with Miss Grimshaw's secretary, Pauline Faulkner."

"Oh, yes, the doctor's daughter. I live in Gramercy Park, just across the courtyard. Come over now and have tea with me. The muffins are hot and the tea is steeping."

"I'd be glad to." The answer to Judy's question was minutes away!

As soon as Amelia opened the door, Judy knew Pauline's preconceived notions about Miss Grimshaw's friends were wrong. The slender woman before her was clothed in brilliant purple and carried herself regally. Her dark, flashing eyes and wide smile offered a warm welcome. Judy couldn't imagine this woman being friends with the brown-clad, matronly figure of Miss Grimshaw. She couldn't even picture the two women standing next to each other.

"Please come in. Our private tea party is ready!"

Music was playing, and Judy recognized the words of a new Christmas carol, "Feliz Navidad." Judy's lively hostess sang along with the words as she led Judy into an elegant sitting room. "I love this song—half Spanish and half English, just like me!" she laughed. "I keep playing it even though some consider Christmas to be over. But I don't want to be distracted by music while we visit," Amelia added, removing the record from the phonograph.

She motioned for Judy to sit down where a silver tea tray was filled and waiting. "Tell me, how you know Emily?"

"I went to her office on my first visit to New York City," Judy said.

"So you're an author?"

"No." Judy didn't know what to say. It seemed silly to explain that she and her friends were intrigued by Dale Meredith and hoped to find him at his literary agent's office.

"From your lack of details I bet there is a good story. Come on, let it out," urged her hostess.

"Pauline, another girlfriend, and I saw Dale Meredith on the bus to New York and wanted to meet him. Dale dropped a telegram from Emily Grimshaw. I looked her up in the phone book and went to her office in hopes of meeting him. She offered me a job, the one Pauline now has. That was several years ago, back when I was in high school." Judy didn't want Amelia to think she would pull a stunt like that now.

"So you landed the job but not the eligible bachelor."

"True, but Irene, my other friend, did marry Dale."

"I've met Irene and love her voice. I always thought she was rather young to run in Dale's circle of friends. It is nice to know how they met. Now we still have to find someone just right for Pauline. The man who gave me the doll might work."

This was the opening Judy wanted. "Did he seem suitable for her?"

"I'm not sure. He seems rich enough, but he may not look the part. Pauline has never mentioned it, and of course she wouldn't, but I suspect she is looking for the traditional tall, dark, and handsome. I bet it was hard for Pauline to lose Dale to Irene." Judy was surprised at this woman's insight. Maybe Amelia and Miss Grimshaw were compatible after all. Emily Grimshaw was certainly astute.

"Then I guess he has light-colored hair?" asked Judy.

"Yes, the color of sand. He is the kind of man who will seem young even when he is wrinkled like me."

"He sounds like my husband," said Judy. She wished she had her wallet with her so she could show Peter's photo to Amelia.

"I have only known him a few days, but he seems like a friend. He's that kind of person."

Judy thought, He may be that kind of opportunist, but kept her suspicions to herself.

"He was so thoughtful to give me the doll," Amelia continued. "He saw my collection and offered it right away. He said it was sitting in the bottom of a cabinet and needed to be enjoyed. It belonged to his grandmother, but as a single man, he had no one to appreciate it. I'll show it to you as soon as we finish our tea."

"And he gave it to you recently?" asked Judy.

"The other night when it snowed again. He had promised and didn't let the weather deter him. I like that in a man. He was late arriving, but it wasn't his fault, of course. His taxi was in a minor accident, and he had to wait for another one. We had a nice visit, and I mentioned Dr. Faulkner. Of course, I must confess that I was also thinking of Pauline when I made the comment. At her age, she can't keep holding out for dark and handsome. I mentioned her to him, discreetly of course." Amelia hesitated then said, "You confessed your little trick with Dale, so I'll even admit that I pointed her out to him the first time we met."

"How did you meet him?" asked Judy.

"He was walking in the neighborhood at the same time I was walking Chica, my dog, and also the same time Pauline was coming home from work. He mentioned that he was tired of working on Wall Street. He preferred helping people instead of large corporations."

"So you asked him for financial advice?" prodded Judy.

"He would be a nice change from the stuffy money manager hired by my late husband. I told Emily she should give this young man a chance. She has money that needs careful managing because of her mother's health problems. She was skeptical at first. Last night she bombarded me with questions. I kept telling her that if he takes us on he would be doing us a favor."

Judy doubted the truth of those words. The UnPeter was clever, very clever. Was he using stolen goods, such as her dolls and the Frozen Tear necklace, to gain the confidence of his next victims? Were his gifts an opening to seniors' investments and pensions?

As soon as they finished eating, Amelia stood and motioned for Judy to follow her. "My dolls are in the next room. I keep them under glass and out of direct sunlight."

Judy wasn't planning to keep her dolls under glass, but she made a mental note to place them on a wall away from sunlight. She hoped they would be found and returned.

"My newest acquisition is the one on the left. Isn't her red sash lovely, and the dress is in such good condition for the age. The hair . . ."

Judy didn't want to disillusion this charming woman, but the doll in the red dress looked too familiar. "I had a similar doll stolen last week," Judy said. "Do you mind if I look at it more closely? My grandmother sewed names on her dolls' chemises."

"Oh, my! I hope you don't think this one is yours, but go ahead. I certainly don't want you to think I have your doll."

If Amelia was miffed, her voice didn't show it. She opened the glass door and gently set the doll on a nearby table.

Judy lifted the dress and looked underneath. "See, here's the name. Phoebe."

"And that was the name of your grandmother's doll?" asked Amelia.

"I had a similar doll stolen last week," Judy said.
"Do you mind if I look at it more closely?"

"I'll have to ask my mother. She said she would recognize the name."

"I hope you are wrong because I've recommended this young man to several friends," worried Amelia.

"I may not be sure of the name, but I am fairly certain it's my doll. I'm sorry," said Judy. "What's the name of the man who gave her to you?"

"Alfred Thompson."

"Thompson!" gasped Judy. "Are you sure?"

Let me give you his business card. It only lists a phone number under his name. His answering service picks up his calls, but he always calls me back."

On the short walk back to the Faulkners' home, Judy considered the new pieces to the puzzle. She finally had a name for the man they had called the UnPeter, Alfred Thompson! Thompson was the same as Peter's birth name, and Peter had confirmed that the suspect was related to him. Now she was convinced that she and the FBI wanted the same man. Was she interfering in FBI business to hunt the man who had violated her home? She didn't think so. As far as she was concerned, Mr. Thompson was fair game. Didn't she have a right to find her grandmother's...no, her own possessions?

CHAPTER XXI

Return to the
Vincenzo Neighborhood

As soon as Judy entered the Faulkners'
home, she hurried upstairs to the privacy of the
guestroom to call the new number Peter had given
her. Surely, the doll discovery and Alfred Thompson's phone number would help him. Judy was disappointed when, as in the past, she had to leave
her information with another FBI agent. Hanging
up the phone, she noticed a message on the table,
"Mrs. Bolton called and said to tell you Sarah and
Phoebe."

She pulled Miss Grimshaw's note from her
pocket and telephoned Amelia. Judy's newest
friend took the news well.

"I'm sorry. It's always sad to find that one's
trust has been misplaced. Shall I bring your doll

over?" asked Amelia.

"No, just wait until the FBI contacts you," Judy advised. I have already notified them, and they should call you with instructions."

"Thank you for saving my nest egg and Emily's as well. I hope you can come by and see me again before you leave."

"I'll try," Judy said.

"Good. We need to put our heads together and find a new man for Pauline. Bye now."

Honey called from the adjoining sitting room. "I've figured it out."

"What do you mean?" asked Judy.

"Remember I told you something was wrong with the house? I've been staring at my drawing and it finally hit me. Draperies cover every window. Ma always kept the curtains open so she could keep an eye on the street. I don't know if she was watching out for the police or keeping up with the neighbors' business. Probably both."

"That is strange," said Judy.

"I think so too," said Honey. "I don't know why I am so worried, but I am. I wish someone could find out what is going on."

"I don't think I'm the person," said Judy.

"You don't have to be the one," said Honey. "You didn't say so, but I know you weren't happy that I decided to visit my old neighborhood and the Vincenzos."

"No, I wasn't, but I'm proud of you for fac-

ing your 'ghost,' as you call it. You could have
kept burying your feelings, but you chose a better,
harder way."

"Thanks, Judy."

Pauline's entrance diverted the subject.

"Did you know that Amelia is a neighbor?"
asked Judy. "She lives across the courtyard."

"I know almost everyone in that section and
can't think of anyone named Amelia. What does
she look like?"

"She's very slender with vibrant, brown eyes,
and she has an elegant way about her."

"It must be Mrs. Cabral," said Pauline. "She
fancies herself a matchmaker."

"The very one," Judy confirmed.

"I didn't know her first name, but I do know
her dog's name is Chica. I see her walking her dog
as I'm coming home from work. Tell me about
your visit while we eat. Mary has lunch ready."

"Lunchtime means I should be leaving to meet
Sylvia," said Judy.

The entire way to Sloan's Diner, Judy wondered how the Vincenzos fit in with Alfred Thompson. Was their involvement a coincidence or even
nonexistent? Judy knew how easily she jumped
to conclusions. Peter didn't seem concerned about
the Vincenzos' visitor, and he hadn't asked her
to stay away from Honey's neighborhood. To be
fair, he didn't know she planned to return.

"I'm sorry I'm late. I wasn't watching the

time," Judy told her dark-haired friend, who was waiting.

"I haven't been here long. I wasn't watching the stops, or rather I was paying too much attention to the people around me and not enough attention to where I was supposed to get off."

"Well, we both made it. Have you ordered?" asked Judy.

"Yes. I felt funny just sitting here. I hope you don't mind," said Sylvia.

"Not at all. Pauline's neighbor fed me a second breakfast so I don't need more food. Do you have a strategy?"

"I have the questionnaire and will say I have to personally meet Mrs. Vincenzo to obtain the answers. At a minimum, we get to talk to a household member."

"Where do I come in?" asked Judy.

"You will be my assistant and record the answers. I brought a clipboard for you to use and a brochure that explains art therapy. You can hand over the brochure. It will make us look more official."

"I can do that. The hardest part will be convincing her sons to let us inside," said Judy.

"I think they will cooperate. Participants in this study can't be paid, but some businesses have offered nice incentives. Mike thinks his brothers will take the bait."

"I don't remember hearing that last night,"

said Judy.

"He mentioned it when he called this morning."

Judy identified the correct house quickly, and Honey was right, the drapes were closed in all the windows. The girls looked at each other for a moment before Sylvia rang the doorbell. After a long pause, the door opened a crack and a face appeared. Judy could see the similarity between this man and Mike Vincenzo. Which brother was he? she wondered.

"What do you want?"

"I understand Mrs. Vincenzo sustained a fall several years ago and has not recovered enough to leave her home," said Sylvia.

"Right. I'm Tony, the one in charge of Ma's treatment. Who told you about her condition? The clinic?"

"I only gather information to see if patients meet the criteria for our research," explained Sylvia. "We offer incentives, of course, if your mother participates. I would like to ask Mrs. Vincenzo a few questions to see if she qualifies for art therapy."

Tony hesitated, but his glance at the clipboard made the door open a little wider. "Is this required for her to keep receiving benefits? I have to leave for a business meeting in an hour." Judy wondered if he was hedging.

"This won't take long," encouraged Sylvia. "I

am sure you are interested in every opportunity to help your mother."

Judy could tell Tony was conflicted. Was he hiding something?

"Local businesses have donated coupons and gift certificates for the participants," Judy told him as she handed him a brochure. "May we see your mother?"

Sylvia was right. The brochure and incentives did the trick.

"Come in." Tony led them up a steep, narrow staircase covered with threadbare carpet and opened a door by the landing. "This is Ma's room."

Although it was the middle of the day, the woman they found seated in a tattered armchair was still dressed in her nightclothes. She appeared to be in her 50s, neither fat nor thin, with dark, gray-streaked hair and coal-black eyes. "May I ask you a few questions, Mrs. Vincenzo?" Sylvia began.

CHAPTER XXII

Alone with Mrs. Vincenzo!

"WHAT do you think?" Sylvia asked when the routine interview was completed and the girls were back on the street.

"I'll tell you as soon as we are out of sight."

Judy led Sylvia to the corner where Honey had stood to view her "backyard" and stopped. "No one can see us from here, especially with the windows covered," said Judy. "I think the woman has more than a physical injury. I think she is scared as well as troubled. I didn't want anything to do with the Vincenzos, but now I am intrigued. I wonder what she would have told us if Tony hadn't been there. This is a real mystery, and I want to solve it, even if it has nothing to do with Alfred Thompson."

"Alfred Thompson? Who is he?" asked Sylvia.

"That's another mystery. The real question is, what to do next? I want to go back, and the sooner, the better."

"So do I. However, if Mrs. Vincenzo is chosen for a follow-up visit, it won't be until next week or even later," explained Sylvia.

"I want to return now, but it would look too suspicious," said Judy.

"I wonder if Tony was telling the truth about going to a meeting."

"If he's gone, Mrs. Vincenzo might answer the door, especially if she looks out and sees it is us. Are you willing to go back?" asked Judy.

"I'm willing to try if Tony's gone," answered Sylvia. "He frightens me."

"Let's give him some time," suggested Judy. "We can walk slowly around the block, and then call on Honey's neighbor. From her front window, we might see him leave."

Judy rang Mrs. Goldin's doorbell and explained that they had just visited Mrs. Vincenzo.

"I'm relieved that you saw Marie today. Is she alright?"

Judy didn't know how to answer, but she didn't have to because Mrs. Goldin kept talking. "I saw Tony leave just after you two left."

Judy realized that Mrs. Goldin had witnessed their visit. She obviously kept tabs on the neighbors.

"Then we may go back and visit with Mrs. Vincenzo some more," said Sylvia.

"I'm sure she will be glad of the company."

When they were back outside, Judy said, "Some people might consider Mrs. Goldin a busybody, but I think she has a good heart."

"Mike said the same thing."

The girls went across the street and rang the Vincenzo doorbell numerous times. "Let's try the back door. Maybe it's unlocked," suggested Sylvia. "I am always forgetting to lock the back door. It drives Mom crazy."

Unfortunately, the back door was locked tight and had a dead bolt as well.

"Maybe a window is unlocked," suggested Judy. Back on the narrow stoop at the top of the steep steps, Judy tried the low window to her right. It was painted shut. She was jiggling the one to the left of the entryway when Sylvia cried out, "I opened the door!"

Judy turned and saw the front door ajar. "What did you do?"

"It was locked but not pulled tight enough to catch," said Sylvia. "Mike said Tony was careless."

"You and Mike seem to be doing a lot of talking lately," teased Judy.

Sylvia blushed. "Let's go inside."

It was hard to see inside the dark house. Fewer lights were on than earlier. "Living in this darkness would give me the creeps," confided Sylvia. She reached to pull back the heavy drapes.

Judy stopped her. "If we open the curtains, we'll give ourselves away."

Judy bumped against a table standing by the steps. Both girls froze to see if the sound was noticed. Even if Tony were gone, another Vincenzo brother might be in the house. After listening a few moments, Judy gave a signal, and they crept upstairs. Judy knocked on Mrs. Vincenzo's door.

When the knock went unanswered, Judy opened the door. Mrs. Vincenzo flinched at the unexpected noise.

"We didn't mean to frighten you," Sylvia reassured her. "We came back to see if you were alright."

Judy wasn't sure the woman believed Sylvia. She looked from one girl to the other without speaking.

"Tony isn't here," said Judy. "I think he went to a meeting. Can we help you?"

Mrs. Vincenzo shook her head.

Had they returned and risked being caught for nothing? Judy decided to plunge ahead. "We know something is wrong. Please let us assist you."

"You can't," was the reply.

"We might be able to," said Judy. "Rose is my best friend, and we helped her."

Although "Rose" flowed easily from Judy's

mouth, she felt like she was talking about a person separate from her dear sister-in-law. Was that how Honey felt when Mrs. Goldin called her "Rose?"

Judy's risky words burst through the barrier in an unexpected way.

"Rose, sweet Rose," sobbed Mrs. Vincenzo. "I just wanted to help her."

"I don't understand." Judy was puzzled. Mrs. Vincenzo had not done anything to benefit Honey. Quite the contrary!

"I loved Rose," the older woman continued. "No one ever took her place. Not even if she was pretty and useful." She repeated, "No one ever took her place."

Judy inferred that Mrs. Vincenzo was talking about helping the real Rose, the one buried in the church graveyard. Honey had not taken Rose's place in the mother's heart. However, Judy didn't understand the remark about helping Rose, or did she?

"Do you mean helping Rose get a decent burial?" asked Judy.

"You know about that?" Mrs. Vincenzo looked frightened.

"Yes, you buried your own daughter and pretended it was little Grace Thompson," said Judy.

"I have suffered so much from that decision." Mrs. Vincenzo seemed anxious to explain. "One day, both babies were weak and had high fevers.

By the next day Grace was better, but little Rose died. I loved Rose. I tried to forget what had happened, and I did for a while, that is until I lost Rose a second time. Now I don't have either one. All I have is a grave with the wrong name. I should have known that Grace couldn't replace Rose."

Judy had to try again, not just for Honey and Mike's sake, but for the sake of this woman who was still suffering from her past choices. "We thought you could use some assistance and came back," she said.

"I'm not used to people helping me. All my life I've had to help myself."

Judy's pity had limits. Help yourself to other people's possessions, she thought.

"Let us help you now," offered Sylvia.

"How can you? Tony's in charge."

There wasn't time to elaborate because, just then, they heard heavy footsteps coming up the stairs. Judy braced herself for a storm that did not appear. After what seemed like minutes, but must have been seconds, they heard the slam of a distant door. Tony, if it was him, didn't intend to check on his mother right away.

"We might be able to sneak out if you think it's best," whispered Sylvia when it became obvious that they were safe for the moment.

Common sense told Judy that she and Sylvia should leave, but Judy wavered. She didn't want to abandon Mrs. Vincenzo. However, Judy remembered seeing the deep scars that Tony had inflicted when Honey had opposed his will.

Judy also had to consider Sylvia. Deep down Judy knew she hadn't played fair with her friend. Sylvia had accompanied Judy without knowing the cruelty of the Vincenzo family or that a man being watched by the FBI might have been in the house the previous day. It would be better to leave and bring back help. Dr. Bolton could advise Judy about Mrs. Vincenzo's condition.

Both girls heard music coming from a distant room. Judy cracked the door and looked out. The chance to leave undetected seemed optimal.

"We want to help and we'll be back," Judy promised before they slipped out of the room and down the dark stairway.

CHAPTER XXIII

Irene's Open House

"I promised her I would be back to help," said Judy.

"You know how I feel about promises," Peter said. For the first time since coming to New York, Judy had not been forced to leave a message with another agent. Peter had been available when she called.

"What else could I have done, and I can't break my promise! Mrs. Vincenzo needs to know she can trust someone."

"You are not breaking your promise, just modifying it," Peter reasoned. "As soon as I hang up the phone, I will have someone check on Mrs. Vincenzo."

"As long as she knows that I kept my word," insisted Judy.

"I wish you hadn't gone inside in the first place."

"I'm glad we did. Are you mad at me?" teased Judy.

"Would it do any good?" sighed Peter.

"Probably not."

"I will do my best to make sure you have an opportunity to see Mrs. Vincenzo again," assured Peter. "Just not at the house and not now. Please, Judy. It might be dangerous."

Judy knew Peter was right. That was why she had left when she thought Tony had returned. "I won't go back without you," Judy agreed.

"If Honey's around, I want to speak with her for a moment."

"She's gone to meet Horace at the bus station," said Judy.

"Good. I am glad Horace will be with you. I'll call you again when I have a chance. Please take care."

As it turned out, Judy was also glad that Horace was around. When the couple returned to the Faulkners', he came upstairs ahead of Honey.

"I'm not sure about how much to share with Honey," Judy confided when she finished telling Horace about the conversation with Mrs. Vincenzo.

"Do you want me to tell Honey what you learned?" asked Horace.

"Would you?" Judy was relieved. "You will know what to say and what to leave out."

"Sure," Horace said and headed downstairs to find Honey.

That settled, Judy went back to choosing a warm outfit for the evening. A grate and firewood had been placed in the center of the roof garden and preparations made for a fire to be started after dinner. Colored Christmas lights were strung all the way across the ledge. It reminded Judy of the night years ago when Japanese lanterns had been hung for Irene's rooftop birthday party. Tonight a TV set had been moved outside so that the group could watch the New Year's Eve festivities at Times Square.

"One year when Mother was alive, it was warm enough for us to come out here and look down on the city celebrating the New Year," Pauline had explained. "I will always remember that night. This afternoon Father and I were reminiscing. He suggested a fire so we could sit out here and look down on the city again."

The plans for New Year's Eve must have pushed Judy's afternoon adventure out of Pauline's mind because no questions were asked. Mike, who would have asked a lot of questions, didn't join them after all. He and Sylvia had decided to mingle with the crowd gathered at Times Square. Judy wondered how much Sylvia would tell Mike about Mrs. Vincenzo.

No matter what Peter said, how delicious the dinner was, or how festive the atmosphere on the roof garden, Judy kept thinking about Mrs. Vincenzo. She was glad when midnight passed, and she could finally climb into bed.

The next morning, at a late breakfast, Oliver announced that Peter was on the phone. "Hi, Sweetheart. I was hoping you would be around."

"Where else would I be?" asked Judy.

"On the way to Irene's open house," said Peter.

Judy looked at her watch. "I didn't realize the time, but we aren't leaving until later. Pauline likes to arrive during the middle of the party. She says she sees the first guests right before they leave, those that come when she does and the latecomers as she starts out the door."

"It sounds like she has open houses down to a science," laughed Peter.

"She definitely socializes more than we do! I've only been to the open houses at the Farringdon-Petts'."

"I know you were upset about Mrs. Vincenzo last night, so I wanted you to know she is receiving care," Peter assured her. "Now you can stop feeling guilty."

"You know me so well. I didn't enjoy last

night for worrying," Judy confessed, and then told Peter about the festivities on the roof garden.

"I can just picture it," said Peter. "We celebrated there the night Irene returned after she had been missing for so long."

"Wouldn't it be nice if we could do something together to celebrate the New Year," said Judy wistfully.

"You might just get your wish sooner than you think. Now let me talk to Horace before I have to go."

Her brother and husband spoke briefly, and shortly afterward Horace left with Honey. All he told Judy was, "Don't wait for us. We'll meet you at the Merediths' party."

"How did Peter know about Irene's open house?" Judy wondered while she and the Faulkners rode the train out to Long Island. Had he been back at the farmhouse and opened Irene's Christmas card without her? No, Peter wouldn't do that. Maybe someone at the Faulkners had told him. Judy thought about the morning's conversation with Peter. Wait. He had said, "You might get your wish sooner than you think." Peter wanted to surprise her by coming to Irene's open house!

The Merediths' home was low, rambling, and recently built to suit its new owners. She and Peter had spent last Christmas with Dale and Irene and their daughter, Judy Irene, who was now in nursery school. Judy was pleased to see that

again Dale had strung outdoor colored lights in
the shape of a Christmas tree. She remembered
last Christmas Eve when she had helped hang ornaments on the Merediths' living room tree and
later fallen asleep on the sofa while waiting for
Peter to return. Would her reunion with Peter be
at the same place this holiday?

"Hi, Judy, Happy New Year! I was wondering
where you were," greeted Flo Gardner, a friend
Judy had met through Pauline and Irene.

"Pauline likes to be a little more than fashion-
ably late," smiled Judy.

"Then you didn't come with Peter?" asked
Flo. "I wanted to say hello, but he seemed eva-
sive. I wondered if you were on the trail of another mystery."

"The only mystery I want to solve right now
is the location of my husband," said Judy. "Where
is he?"

"In the library talking with one of Dale's
friends," Flo informed her.

"Thanks, I'll look there first."

The library was crowded, and Judy didn't see
Peter. She could usually spot him easily in a group
because of his height. Why hadn't she asked Flo
how long ago it had been since she had seen Peter?
Judy made her way into the dining room. Maybe
Peter had circled back to get more food. On the
way, she bumped into Honey, Horace, and Mike.

Honey touched her arm and whispered in her

ear. "I just came from seeing Ma. Can we find a private place for us all to talk?"

Judy welcomed the news. "Let's slip into little Judy's room. I know Irene wouldn't mind."

"I know I've gotten older, but I wasn't expecting Ma to age or to change so much these past years." Honey began. "She seemed frail and less belligerent. Now I can understand that Ma was traumatized when the real Rose died unexpectedly. My sudden disappearance brought back all of those memories. I think it also brought regrets. The combination was just too much for her, and she started withdrawing."

"Was it hard talking with Mrs. Vincenzo?" asked Judy.

"No, because I felt sorry for her and because Peter had already spoken with her. She knew that I had discovered my real identity and was living with my grandparents. She was surprised my grandparents wanted me because when Grandma came to get Peter, she never asked about me. Vine must not have told her that Peter had a baby sister. Ma claims she would have confessed if Grandma had asked for me. I want to believe that, Judy."

"You are more charitable than I am. Did you see Peter?" asked Judy.

"No. He had already left, but Horace and Mike were with me. I don't blame Ma for switching the babies. There's no use crying over the past or imagining what might have been. I've forgiven

her, Judy, and I asked her to forgive me for running away and never contacting her."

"You ran to save your life!" exclaimed Judy.

"Yes, but I could have dropped her a note to
tell her I was alive. I can see what you think, Judy,
but I had to forgive her for my sake, not necessarily for her sake. And I had to ask forgiveness
too. Forgiveness is what makes me free from the
past."

Mike put his arm around Honey's shoulder.
"She shouldn't have switched the babies, Sis, but
I'm glad you were my sister when I was growing
up. If Red offers me the job, I'm going to take it
so we can stay close. There is no need for me to
stay here. Ma will get the help she needs, and we
can check on her regularly."

Horace turned to Honey. "I'll bring you to
New York whenever I can," he offered. "I'll ask
for more time off if you want to stay through next
week."

"I don't think so," said Honey. "Right now, I
just want to think about what I've learned these
last few days."

"The visit wasn't all negative," added Mike.
"Ma was able to tell Honey some information
about her parents."

"I wrote everything down. I didn't want
to forget a word because I've longed to know
such details about my parents. There was this
song about Slippery Sam from Oil City that my

father used to sing. Ma remembered the beginning lines." Honey pulled out her sketchbook. "Here they are. 'I'll tell a story if you're willing, about Slippery Sam who started drilling.'"

"That's cute. I wonder how the song ends," said Judy.

"Me too," said Honey.

"I was just looking for Peter before you told me your news," said Judy.

"You mean he's here?" exclaimed Honey.

"Flo saw him, and he hinted at it this morning. Did one of you tell him about the open house?" asked Judy.

"Not me," said Honey.

"I didn't talk to him until this morning," Horace said. "All he told me was that it was safe for Honey to see Mrs. Vincenzo and that she had been moved to a medical facility."

"Maybe he stopped back at Dry Brook Hollow at some point and opened the Christmas cards, although that isn't like him," said Judy. "We always open them together."

"Ask him yourself," said Horace. "I just saw the back of his head."

Judy turned in time to get a glimpse of a man ducking into Irene and Dale's bedroom.

CHAPTER XXIV

Alone with Alfred Thompson

JUDY'S hopes were crushed again. Instead of Peter, the thief who bore a strange likeness to her husband was standing before her. Although Judy had been searching for this man, she was disappointed to see him now.

"It's you again!" The intruder was startled, but not enough to keep him from quickly turning on his most charming smile.

"It's nice to see you…Judy, if I remember correctly."

Judy decided that following his lead would yield better results than hostility and accusations. "Small world," she replied in her sweetest voice. "I didn't realize you knew Dale and Irene."

"I met them through a mutual friend, and

they were nice enough to invite me."

The invitation! When she had sat at her kitchen table and looked over the itemized list of missing Wedgwood and dolls, the table had been bare. Nothing had been moved out of the way to make room for the police papers, certainly not Christmas cards.

Judy silently scolded herself. Why didn't I realize the cards were missing from the table? Honey and Pauline both mentioned that the invitation to Irene's party was in their Christmas cards.

Aloud, Judy asked, "What are you doing in here?" She kept her voice light.

"I didn't mean to startle you. I needed to make a phone call, and Irene offered her room."

Judy chided herself again. I should have thought of the cards while Pauline was clipping address labels. Oh, no, the address labels! Because Dale was a famous mystery writer and Irene appeared on television weekly, it was likely their names would be recognized. Even if he hadn't, the waitress at the Brass Kettle had called Irene the Golden Girl.

Judy wondered if Pauline's return address had also drawn Alfred Thompson to Gramercy Park, and therefore to Amelia Cabral. Probably so. The addresses of wealthy people, the stolen photo, and the party invitation all combined to create a great opportunity for a thief.

"I'll leave so you can make your phone call,"

said Judy. "I wandered in here by accident."

When Judy turned to go, she saw, in the reflection of the mirror over Irene's dresser, the contents of Irene's jewelry box, dumped out on the bed. Was that why this man had ducked in here? Unfortunately, Judy gave herself away when her eyes lingered on the image.

The criminal dropped his charm. Before Judy could react, he gripped her arm, and with his foot kicked the door closed. "No reason to leave now. I was meaning to look you up so we could talk."

"Talk about what?" demanded Judy, dropping her friendliness. "How you robbed my house?"

Her question was ignored. "Play along with me, and I'll make sure your friends stay out of trouble. I must admit, I was surprised to discover your illegal activities.... You look so innocent," he added, chuckling.

"I don't know what you mean," protested Judy.

"Yes, you do." Alfred Thompson looked amused. "I had just pulled up to visit a client when I recognized Miss Faulkner leaving 120 Gramercy Park. This client had previously pointed out your friend to me. She thought we would make a good match—don't you agree?"

His sarcastic tone infuriated Judy, but she managed to hold her tongue. She recollected that Pauline and Mike had been the last to enter the taxi and that Mike had commented on a passenger alighting from another cab. She was tempted to ask, "Were you planning to rob my friend too?" Instead she waited to see what else he would say.

"Obviously I was interested in why Miss Faulkner and her pals were out on such a night. I hopped back in my cab and followed you. As soon as I saw everyone examining the names on gravestones, I knew you were looking for opportunities."

"Opportunities? At a cemetery?"

"Don't play with me. I don't know what your friends' game is, but I know only a criminal would be systematically checking gravestones at night. They are the best places to harvest names and their corresponding dates of birth. Once you have them, the rest is easy. You can send off for a copy of a birth certificate, and you know all the doors that piece of paper will open: falsified passports, driver's licenses, you name it. The dates of death tell you which families might have come into money over the past few years. Gravestones are a gold mine."

"That's the craziest thing I ever heard of!" declared Judy.

"Don't bother denying it. We both know it's true. I shared a cell with a man who bragged about the cemetery trick."

Judy tried another tactic. "What do you want from me?" she asked.

"Use your husband's position to make things

easier for me. Who better than an FBI agent to make sure I can conduct my business without interference. Oh, yes, the nosy neighbor filled me in."

"FBI!" Judy gasped. She had jumped to conclusions and told Mrs. Goldin that this man was a government official, but she had never mentioned the FBI.

"You mean Mrs. Goldin?" she asked incredulously.

"If Mrs. Goldin was the blonde with the cookies. She wondered why you and I weren't home earlier that day and asked if I had FBI business to do on a weekend."

Judy was flabbergasted. Holly had seen this man, not Peter. Judy could understand Flo being fooled, as she had only seen Peter for a few hours on Fire Island last November and had not talked with him today. But Holly! How had Holly been fooled?

Her shocked silence must have led the criminal to think she was considering his offer. "Remember, I know where you live, and I look enough like your husband that I can also put him at risk. It wouldn't do any good for the FBI to find out that Agent Dobbs and his lovely wife are involved in criminal activities. So," he concluded, "How do I get in touch with your husband? The sooner the better."

Judy couldn't agree more. The sooner Peter found this person, the better.

"I expected he would be here, but he must be out of town. Tell me how my husband can contact you," said Judy.

"I'd rather contact him, and there's no time like the present."

"Well, I do have a phone number, but I can't guarantee he'll answer," said Judy.

"You'll just have to take your chances. Get him on the phone, and I'll do the talking. And hold the phone where we can both hear." This man may have sounded like Peter earlier, but this voice filled with malice did not resemble the voice she loved.

Judy dialed the easy-to-remember FBI number. The phone was answered with a simple "Hello," not "FBI Field Office." Had she remembered the number correctly?

"May I please speak with Peter Dobbs?"

"He's on the road, but I can give him a message," a woman replied.

"This is his wife, Judy." She paused. What kind of coded message could she send?

"Are you at the Merediths'?" asked the voice when Judy remained silent.

"Yes, with someone who insists he speak with Peter about . . . investments."

"If you'll be there for a while, I'll do my best to have Peter call you back."

Alfred Thompson shook his head.

"That's okay. He just indicated that he can

talk with Peter another time," said Judy.

"Anything else you would like me to tell Mr. Dobbs?" asked the woman.

Judy's captor tightened his grip on her arm and hissed in her ear, "End the call now!"

Judy only had time to say, "I have to go," before Alfred used his free hand to push the button to disconnect the call.

"Now straighten the jewelry box, and make it snappy," he said as he dropped her arm and blocked the door with his body. "Next we're going out there, and you are going to introduce me as a relative of your husband and an investment advisor. Pick someone wealthy because I don't have to remind you that I call the shots."

"You don't expect me to allow you to exploit my friends!" exclaimed Judy.

"I don't exploit my clients, and I'm on my way to becoming a very successful investment counselor," the man objected. "I'm offering you a great opportunity! Pick the right person, and we can all make a bundle. Remember, you have more than one friend to protect, as well as your husband. Accidents can happen to anyone."

"Alright," agreed Judy. She knew exactly who she would pick.

CHAPTER XXV

Peter's Heritage

"My brother is always interested in ways to make more money," Judy said as they entered the dining room. "He's probably by the food." She looked around. "I was right. There he is."

"Hi, Horace," she called out.

Judy saw Alfred Thompson's face light up and wondered if he remembered that Horace was a diamond expert who had given Honey "valuable works of art."

Horace choked on the bite he had taken and looked around for a napkin to wipe some sauce off his fingers. "I didn't mean to startle you," Judy said. To make sure Horace understood the role she was playing, she continued, "I'm sorry about the bridge game. I know I was mad, but brothers are more important than a card game. I've decided to forget our silly argument."

Horace quickly took on his new role. "Then I'll do the same." He gave his sister a magnanimous grin.

"I don't think you've met Alfred Thompson. He is one of Peter's distant relatives and an investment advisor. I know you would like to build your portfolio before you build your new house. Mr. Thompson might be able to help you."

"That would be great." Horace glanced protectively at Honey. "I can't talk here though. Judy, can you keep Honey occupied while we speak elsewhere?"

"I prefer that your sister stay with us," said the phony investment advisor.

"My investments are none of my sister's business, and I intend to keep it that way," said Horace. "Excuse us, Judy."

"Certainly, and in case you are interested, I saw a table full of sweets in the library."

"Then we'll go there," said Horace. "Thanks, Judy. I owe you one."

Judy could just imagine the front-page story Horace would write about this adventure, or maybe it would become the plot of his next novel. As Honey had said, Horace was a treasure. His quick thinking had given her an escape and kept the criminal away from Honey, who might be endangered or say something to create suspicion.

Could Horace stall long enough for Judy to summon help?

Judy looked around. Now that Irene's bedroom was empty, it seemed the safest place to call the Field Office.

The same woman answered her call.

"May I speak with Peter Dobbs?" Judy asked.

"He's not here, but I gave him your message. Are you still at the Merediths'?"

"Yes."

"Please hold for a minute." Judy was put on hold before she could give more information and then dismissed with, "Thank you for calling."

Judy was furious! Did this woman think she was just a bothersome wife? What should she do next? It would be fruitless to call back because the same person would answer. Judy decided to watch Horace's conversation from a distance, but was detained by some of Irene's former neighbors whom Judy had met last Christmas. When she was finally free, Flo stopped her. Would she ever make it to the library?

"Your husband is looking for you," said Flo.

"He's not my husband," objected Judy.

"Who's not your husband?" asked the voice she loved. If she had remaining doubts, they were erased as soon as Peter's arms encircled her.

"This time I'm happy to be wrong," said Judy.

"Can you point me and my friends in the right direction?"

Judy did as requested.

"Now, I need food more than questions," said Peter when he returned alone a few minutes later.

"I'll fix you a plate and pile it high." Judy knew Peter wasn't hungry as much as he was reminding her that he couldn't divulge confidential information with so many guests nearby.

As soon as they were alone, Judy told Peter about her conversation with Alfred Thompson. Later she answered questions from Peter's superiors. However, Judy's own questions were not answered until that night. With Horace staying at the Faulkners, the house was too full to add another guest. Peter suggested splurging on a nearby hotel that overlooked the city's holiday lights.

"This makes up for last night," said Judy. "I couldn't enjoy Pauline's rooftop party because I kept thinking about Mrs. Vincenzo."

"Are you satisfied about her now?" asked Peter.

"Yes."

"Although I wouldn't have wanted you to go back to the Vincenzos', it proved to be helpful for Honey. Who knows when Mrs. Vincenzo would have revealed what happened with Rose."

"What I really want to know now is how you got to Irene and Dale's so fast."

"I was already on my way. We expected our man to attend the open house, but as far as we knew he was still in his hotel room. After you called I was radioed, and his room was checked. Although he was being watched, he managed to give us the slip. Agents in the area were asked to join me at the Merediths'."

"I tried to give you a clue before the call was disconnected."

"You did when you mentioned investments. Your testimony will be valuable, Sweetheart. Our man both gave himself away and added to his charges when he threatened you if you didn't cooperate." Peter shook his head. "I don't know how you do it, but you always manage to remain calm in frightening situations," he added admiringly.

"I'm calm on the outside. At least something good came from that awful experience. I'm glad I could help."

"You helped from the beginning by spotting the accomplice at Brandt's and then in New York. It led the FBI here. New York was not on our radar."

"Our Christmas cards put New York on the radar," said Judy.

"We realized that when we found the cards and some maps in Thompson's hotel room. Irene's and Pauline's neighborhoods were circled."

"So that's how you knew about the open house."

"Yes," Peter replied.

"That means I led him to our home and then

diverted him to New York," sighed Judy.

"Don't be so hard on yourself. Having lunch with our suspect made you suspicious when Emily Grimshaw mentioned an investment counselor. You persisted in following that important clue. Amelia Cabral's information gave us the phone number being used in New York. When Thompson called his answering service, we were able to trace the call to his hotel. His office consisted of his briefcase, which he left in his room while he was out. We found evidence that he was operating a Ponzi scheme. I don't know how it could have worked out better for the FBI. It turned out well for us, too, Sweetheart. Some of your Wedgwood was in his hotel room."

"What is a Ponzi scheme?" asked Judy.

"It is a type of investment fraud using the funds from new investors to pay returns to earlier investors. Thompson sought out wealthy people—lots of them—and convinced them that his jewelry and antiques businesses offered high returns for their investments with little or no risk. He even had colorful brochures printed showing elegant shops and jewelry. But it was all a sham."

"I'm glad we'll have our possessions returned, but what about the people who invested their money with him? Will they get their money back?"

"Unfortunately, there isn't much money to give back to them."

"No wonder he was eager to meet wealthy people," Judy reflected.

"With little or no legitimate earnings, he needed a constant flow of money from new investors to continue, and he supplemented that by fencing stolen property," Peter explained.

"Was he the man at the Vincenzo house?" asked Judy.

"The person Mrs. Goldin saw was one of Tony's pals, who was collecting a gambling debt. He probably showed Tony a gun, not credentials. Now, let's put this topic aside and enjoy our evening together," said Peter.

During the trip back to Dry Brook Hollow the next evening, Judy asked the rest of her questions. "You said that the criminal was related to you, so is Alfred Thompson his real name?" asked Judy.

"Yes, he's my father's youngest half-brother. He's closer to my age than would be expected, given that he is my uncle."

Judy thought for a moment before exclaiming, "He's the man Chief Kelly arrested the night of my Halloween party! If it hadn't been so dark, I might have recognized him in Bradford. I thought he was still in prison."

"He was convicted of the attempted robbery at your house and a few minor burglaries elsewhere, so he only served a short sentence. Unfortunately his time in prison changed him for the worse. That is where he learned about Ponzi schemes. One of my great-uncles, Uncle Jeremy, is willing to stay in touch with Alfred and help him turn his life around this time."

"Uncle Jeremy sounds like a wonderful man," said Judy. "Is he a Thompson?"

"Yes. Uncle Jeremy was my grandfather's brother."

"How did you find him?" asked Judy.

"Because of your clue from the driver's license, we questioned people in Oil City. I wonder if my father mentioned Oil City when I was a child. Why else would it seem so familiar?"

"He did!" cried Judy. "Mrs. Vincenzo told Honey that your father sang a song about Slippery Sam from Oil City."

Peter grinned. "Wow! That's incredible!"

"Honey wrote down what Mrs. Vincenzo remembered," Judy told him. It started out, "'I'll tell a story if you're willing...'"

"'About Slippery Sam who started drilling,'" Peter continued, singing the words.

"'All day long the man would toil,
Till one fine day Old Sam struck oil!
He was rich, his wife was pretty,
Slippery Sam from Oil City.'"

Judy gave Peter an amazed look. "I can't believe you remembered a song from 20 years ago!"

"I didn't until now. Childhood memories must go deep. Knowing that I actually remember something about my father is pretty special."

Judy was eager to hear more. "What else did you learn?"

"Oil City is a small town, and people remembered my family, especially because my grandfather made a fortune in the oil business. Peter Thompson married Pamela Hopkins, and my father, James, was their only son. Everyone I questioned volunteered that my paternal grandparents were both kind and generous."

Judy was leaning against Peter's shoulder, and the road had been lulling her to sleep, but now she sat straight up. "So you were named after your grandfather!"

"Yes," Peter continued. "My grandmother died when my father was only seven."

"How sad," Judy sympathized. "I wonder how a fine man like your grandfather got involved with Vine Thompson."

"Still the 'I wonder' girl," teased Peter. "Uncle Jeremy believes my grandfather was lonely and wanted a mother for his son. They met while my grandfather was on a business trip. Apparently Vine was beautiful and could be charming when she wanted to be."

"The trunk we found in my parents' attic contained lovely clothes," Judy recalled. "I always wondered how the wearer of such gowns could be as ruthless as rumored."

"Apparently my dad's father died soon after

Alfred was born. It was ruled a heart attack, but family members said it was a broken heart from being married to an unloving, greedy woman. At the funeral, Vine Thompson made it clear that she had no interest in taking care of a teenager, so James moved in with Uncle Jeremy.

"I can guess what happened to the family fortune," said Judy.

"Yes, Vine ran through it in five years," said Peter, "And once it was gone, she needed a new source of income. She moved to Farringdon and started her life of crime. My father had just finished high school and went with her. He wanted to spend more time with his half-brothers. By that time, he was old enough to be useful to Vine, so she welcomed him. Growing up with Uncle Jeremy, I bet my father had no idea what Vine was really like."

"James found out quickly because he couldn't have been more than eighteen when he ran off and married your mother. Chief Kelly said he died at age twenty-two." Judy sighed. "How sad. Does it help to know more about your father?"

"Yes, and I received more than facts. Uncle Jeremy gave me some photos and a few items that belonged to my father and grandparents. I have one thing picked out for Honey, and she can have anything else she wants."

"I'm still surprised at the strong resemblance between you and Alfred. I always thought you took after the Dobbs side of the family."

"Not entirely," Peter replied. "Alfred and I are both tall, which apparently comes from the Thompson side."

"Now that I think about it, your Grandpa Dobbs isn't tall," said Judy.

"According to Uncle Jeremy, my Grandfather Thompson was blond and had blue eyes like mine," said Peter.

"Did I tell you Alfred admitted that he had met Holly?" asked Judy.

"When did he meet Holly?"

"The night our house was robbed. Didn't I tell you that Holly said she had come over and given you some cookies?"

"No."

"I guess I was in a hurry to tell you about the robbery so I skipped that part. I thought you had come back to the farmhouse for files or clothes. I don't understand how Holly was fooled," said Judy.

"What exactly did Holly say?" asked Peter.

Judy thought back and answered, "Just that she had handed you some cookies and you thanked her. I assumed that she saw you inside because Eric said the house lights were on."

"I'm surprised that Holly didn't see the difference between me and Alfred—she knows me well."

"That's why I believed her. Oh, wait a

minute," Judy interrupted herself as a new thought occurred to her. "Eric told me that Holly said you were sniffling. I'd like to bet something precious that he was using a big handkerchief, pretending to sniff when he was just hiding his nose and chin that aren't anywhere as nice as yours."

"My nose and chin thank you."

Judy cast an affectionate glance in Peter's direction. "Tell me your paternal grandparents' names again," said Judy.

"Peter Thompson and Pamela Hopkins."

"Peter and Pamela...I like those names," Judy murmured as she returned her head to Peter's shoulder and closed her eyes.

CHAPTER XXVI

Two Announcements

THE next morning Judy awoke in her own bed, with Blackberry curled up at her feet. Outside, the sky was clear, with sunshine reflecting off the fallen snow. The world looked brighter this morning. She was home. Honey and Horace should be home soon, and Mike would follow in a month. Red had been serious about the job offer. Judy walked into the kitchen just as Peter came up from the cellar with his tape measure.

"You're an early bird this morning."

"The early bird catches the worm," Judy quoted, "but the idea of a worm for breakfast doesn't appeal to me."

"Me either," Peter chuckled. "I thought I would surprise you and make the doll shelves

221

right away. The police should be able to return your dolls soon."

"I'm glad you have a project for today because I have my own project," said Judy.

After breakfast, Judy drove into Roulsville and spent the morning shopping, returning in time to prepare sandwiches. When Peter came into the kitchen, he announced, "The shelves are finished. Do you need anything else done?"

"I would like a fire in the fireplace if you don't mind bringing in the wood," suggested Judy.

"I'll do it right after lunch, and then I have to make a quick trip to the Field Office. I'll be back in time for dinner."

"Did you get a call?" asked Judy. "I didn't hear the phone ring."

"I already knew this paperwork had to be filed, but I wasn't going to let it come before building shelves for your dolls. Sometimes FBI work has to take precedence over our time together, but not this time."

After Peter left, Judy only had Blackberry for company as she prepared a celebratory dinner. She and Peter often joked about the unromantic setting of Peter's faltering proposal over a lunch of hamburgers at Joe's Diner. The memory would always be sentimental to Judy because she loved Peter, but tonight she wanted to create both a romantic evening and a lasting memory.

When everything was in the oven, Judy pulled out the embroidered place mats she had received as a shower present. Not only had she been reluctant about using Grandma Smeed's Wedgwood; lately she had been the same way with her wedding gifts. She took the candlesticks from the mantel and placed yellow candles in them. The fire Peter had lit was burning brightly. They would eat by the fireplace in the living room. Everything went smoothly, and she was showered and changed by the time she heard the front door opening.

"It sure smells good in here. What are we celebrating? Being home?" asked Peter.

"More than that," said Judy. "I just need to put the plates on the table, and we can eat."

"I was thinking about your grandparents, Peter and Pamela. Those are nice names. What do you think?" asked Judy after they had filled their plates.

"About my grandparents?" asked Peter.

"No, about the names. Especially the name Pamela. That would be a nice name for a girl," said Judy.

"I thought we were talking about the previous generation. I take it you would rather talk about starting the next generation," said Peter, taking both of Judy's hands in his as blue eyes gazed into gray ones.

"So what do you think of the name Pamela?" Judy asked.

"I think the name is as beautiful you are," said Peter huskily.

Suddenly Judy felt shy. She had planned everything but what to say. Maybe this was how Peter felt at Joe's Diner. To cover her confusion, Judy went into the kitchen, and even though they had barely started dinner, she carried out the dessert she had made. Peter studied her but didn't say a word. When they had eaten a few more bites, he gave Judy an encouraging smile. "Would you like to continue this interesting conversation?" he asked.

"Which conversation?" asked Judy. Had she missed something he had said while she decided how to bring up the subject?

"Starting the next generation," Peter smiled.

"It's already started," Judy blurted out. She immediately felt foolish. This was not how she wanted to tell Peter. She began again with, "What I meant to say," but she couldn't find the rest of the words. It didn't matter because suddenly Peter's arms were encircling her, and he was happily swinging her around the room. Judy knew they would remember this special moment forever.

Although Judy was eager to share her good news, she and Peter decided to make their announcement at a family gathering when Horace and Honey returned from New York.

Two days later, Honey called. Honey's voice told Judy that more good news was coming.

"You won't believe this!" exclaimed Honey.

"Oh, I bet I can," said Judy. "I can tell by the joy in your voice."

"Really?" asked Honey. "Did Peter tell you what Uncle Jeremy gave him?"

Judy was confused by the unexpected topic. She was expecting an official engagement announcement.

"No. Peter mentioned some photos and some things that had belonged to your grandparents. He did say that he had one thing in particular for you."

"Oh, Judy, it is so wonderful. It makes me feel connected to my father's family. Just a minute."

Judy heard Honey talking to someone in the background before she returned to the phone. "Horace says he will drive me right out. You have to see this to believe it."

Judy wondered what could make Honey so excited. Honey and Horace's engagement shouldn't involve Peter's paternal grandparents.

"What took you so long?" Judy asked her brother when the couple finally arrived.

"I'm settling down, which includes being a reformed driver," said Horace with a smile in Honey's direction.

"Where's Peter?" asked Honey.

"Upstairs painting the spare bedroom. We'll have to go up to him because it'll take too long for him to clean up and come down to us."

Judy had not considered the consequences when she had invited her visitors upstairs. Baby fabric for new curtains sat on a chair in the hallway. If that wasn't enough, the pale pink being spread on the walls could have only one meaning. It wasn't any pink. It was baby pink. Peter had offered to repaint the room if their child turned out to be a boy.

Horace grinned when he surveyed the wall that was finished, but Honey was oblivious. "Look, Peter," she said as she grabbed her necklace with her left hand and held it out. "They match."

Judy looked in amazement. There was a second marquise diamond on Honey's left hand. "Wow!" said Peter. "Where did you get the diamond necklace?"

Judy had forgotten that Peter was away when Honey had explained the pre-engagement necklace. Judy was surprised by the ring, not the necklace.

"The stone in the necklace is the one Horace originally chose for my engagement ring."

Honey turned to Judy and held out her left hand. "This diamond belonged to my grandmother."

Judy was confused for a brief moment because her own engagement ring had belonged to Grandma Dobbs. She quickly realized that Honey was referring to the newly discovered Grandmother Thompson.

"And now it's your engagement ring! Congratulations!" Judy hugged first her brother and then his future bride. "Honey, soon you'll be my double sister-in-law."

"That's true, and Peter will be my double brother-in-law," Horace said.

"The ring is beautiful, and it has a history that's rather poignant," said Peter.

Honey turned her hand, watching the diamond sparkle in the sunlight streaming in the window. "My grandfather wanted my grandmother to be buried with her engagement diamond, but Uncle Jeremy thought it was an emotional decision that his brother would later regret. He kept Pamela's ring and, after his brother died, he saved it for my father to give to his bride. When our parents eloped and went to New York, Uncle Jeremy planned to give it to our father when he visited Oil City. He never did visit, so Uncle Jeremy has had the ring all these years.

"He was mighty glad to return the ring to a rightful heir," said Peter. "He brought it to me as soon as he discovered who I was. I showed it to Horace because I knew it was meant for Honey."

"It certainly is," Horace confirmed. "The prongs were worn down, so the jeweler recommended a new mounting."

"We agreed to use the mounting Horace bought for my engagement ring and not reset the other diamond," Honey explained. "Now I have something from both Horace and my grandmother on my finger."

"The necklace is just as important to us," added Horace.

"It will always remind me of our secret promise to each other and the fact that Horace considered my feelings above his own. The thing that amazes me is that my grandparents chose the same diamond cut that Horace did. Can you believe that the diamonds are even the same size? It makes me feel like I am a part of them."

"Something old, something new," repeated Judy from the familiar wedding verse. "I bet that never applied to twin diamonds before."

"Now I just need something borrowed and something blue," said Honey.

"Speaking of blue, why are these walls being covered with pink instead of blue?" asked Horace.

"Because I like the name Pamela. It was the name of Peter and Honey's grandmother. I looked it up today, and it means 'a girl of honeyed sweetness.'"

"Oh! Oh, Judy!" Honey gasped, finally noticing the pink room. "Oh, Peter, a baby, how wonderful! I was so wrapped up in my twin diamonds that I didn't even notice!"

Honey enveloped Judy in a hug and then kissed her brother's paint-splattered cheek.

"I hope Peter Junior likes pink," observed Horace.

"Don't worry. His daddy promised to repaint the room if a baby boy shows up," said Judy. "Right now my husband is indulging me."

"Well how about indulging me in some food. Becoming officially engaged takes energy," said Horace.

"That's a great idea. Let's have a family dinner tonight," suggested Judy. "You can announce your news and then next week Peter and I will announce ours."

"I like the idea of telling our families at the same time, so let's both make announcements tonight," countered Honey. "I don't want to be the center of attention all evening."

Judy didn't want to take away from Honey's special moment. She looked over at Horace, and he indicated that he wanted her to agree with his future wife.

"Okay. We'll do it your way. Usually I wonder what the new year will hold, but this year I know," said Judy.

"You know two special things that will happen this year, but I imagine it won't be long before you start wondering about some new mystery," Peter predicted.

"I like it when we solve mysteries together," Judy smiled, "especially when they have happy endings."

Creating
The Strange Likeness

Margaret Sutton provided hints to the identity of Judy Bolton's latest nemesis in two previous books. In addition to creating the title of *The Strange Likeness*, she also started a plot outline and shared her dreams for Judy, Peter, Horace, and Honey with her family and some of her fans.

Kate Duvall is president of the Phantom Friends, a series-book fan club which began as a discussion group for Judy Bolton fans. Today the group continues to bring Judy Bolton and other series sleuths to life through newsletters and group meetings. Kate was inspired to write this book by her conversations and correspondence with Margaret Sutton. She set the central plot line to address unanswered questions from the original series.

Beverly Hatfield has been a devoted Judy Bolton fan since childhood and enjoys introducing young girls today to this star detective. She brings to the project an in-depth understanding of each of the characters and creates a seamless transition from Margaret's writing to this new edition. Each Judy Bolton mystery was inspired by actual events, and Beverly created clues and settings from real life based on conversations with Sutton's daughter and her own experiences.

Marjorie Sutton Eckstein inherited her mother's creative drive. She illustrated the Gail Gardner nurse series while majoring in art. As a stay-at-home mom she wrote and illustrated stories for children. When her three boys were older, she worked as an artist in fashion, design, and illustration. Now retired from Grumman's art department, she paints to her heart's delight and is a member of the b.j. spoke gallery in Huntington, New York.

Lindsay Sutton Stroh is the executrix of her mother's estate and served as editor and coordinator of *The Strange Likeness*. She contributed several story ideas, including the antique dolls, based on the dolls she inherited from her great-aunt. Lindsay's career has included public relations, fundraising, grant writing, and journalism. She enjoys composing poetry and songs.

CPSIA information can be obtained
at www.ICGtesting.com
Printed in the USA
BVHW04s1319230518
517120BV00002B/194/P